Christmas
with
Southern Living.
1986

**Compiled and Edited by
Nancy Janice Fitzpatrick**

Oxmoor
House.

Library of Congress Catalog Card Number: 84-63032
ISBN: 0-8487-0684-6
ISSN: 0747-7791
Manufactured in the United States of America
First Printing

Executive Editor: Candace Conard Bromberg
Production Manager: Jerry Higdon
Associate Production Manager: Rick Litton
Art Director: Bob Nance

Christmas with Southern Living 1986
Senior Editor: Nancy Janice Fitzpatrick
Editor: Kathleen English
Assistant Editor: Alison Nichols
Foods Editors: Susan Payne, Nancy Nevins
Editorial Assistant: Margaret Allen Northen
Foods Stylist: Beverly Morrow
Artists: Barbara Ball, Diana Smith Morrison
Copy Chief: Mary Jean Haddin
Designer: Carol Middleton

Contents

Christmas Journal

Patterns

Contributors

Introduction

Do you recall some particularly memorable moment of the Christmas season? An experience that, for you, embraced the true meaning of this day? Perhaps you spent a Christmas far from home, a potentially lonely time that was gladdened by a new friend's thoughtfulness. Or it might have been simply the opening of a perfectly chosen gift that made you feel loved and warm all over.

If you've ever known such an occurrence, you probably realize that, although Christmas is essentially miraculous, caring deeds by each of us make it even more wondrous. These acts, reinforcing our beliefs and strengthening the bonds of love and friendship, often become cherished practices that we repeat year after year—our Christmas traditions.

It's never too late to make an effort that may one day become a beloved tradition. Consider, for instance, that, although the birth of Christ was almost 2,000 years ago, the celebration of Christmas as we know it is a relatively recent tradition. In this country, the observance of the holiday was actually banned by New England Puritans in the mid-1600s, as a pagan ritual. (Southern colonials, however, celebrated Christmas with great enthusiasm. And eventually, Alabama was the first state to make December 25 a legal holiday, in 1836.) Even our most popular custom, decorating an evergreen tree, was not common in America until about 150 years ago.

Although you probably have some well-established Christmas traditions, there are many fresh and exciting possibilities within the pages of this book to help make the upcoming holidays the best of times.

We hope you will find here everything you need for all your holiday decorating, gift giving, and entertaining, and that some of these carefully selected ideas will become fond traditions in your home.

Christmas around the South

Define a Southerner. It's as easy as catching a falling star. Even so, it's something passed along, a state of mind that winds throughout this region and beyond. Look at people who've come here from other places, never to leave. Look at Southerners who have moved elsewhere, taking their Southern charm with them. Southerners come from all backgrounds, all corners of the globe. And in this land of rich differences, a journey down the roads and rivers offers glimpses into the qualities that unify.

Life does move at a slower pace in the South. That stereotype is true. Folks here cherish family, food, and celebrations, relishing life's events and drawing them out to their fullest. It's only the particulars that change from place to place.

Some of those particulars are chronicled in "Christmas around the South." In West Virginia, we visit the governor's mansion, where the first family sustains old-style elegance and proudly displays the works of area crafters. Heading south to Louisiana, we view a pocket of culture that has endured despite mass media—that of the Cajuns. And in North Carolina, we see a mansion whose owners gleaned treasures from exotic lands to create an offbeat—but still Southern—brand of opulence. Finally, a pilgrimage to Shakertown, Kentucky, points out just how diverse is this region called the South.

And yet, the diversity poses no contradictions. Southerners are like members of a family, each distinct and each attuned to the others. And those distinctions illustrate both season and sentiment as we travel the South for the holidays.

Greetings from West Virginia

A governor's mansion, in addition to being home to the state's highest official, should also be a source of pride to the people of that state. That's how Governor and Mrs. Arch Moore feel about their home in the capitol complex at Charleston, West Virginia. The house reflects the Moores' personal style with traditionally elegant decorations. But throughout the rooms is evidence of the Moores' pride in their state and its most valuable resource—talented people. Mrs. Moore explains, "We have so many fine craftsmen in our state, and we try to display their work at every opportunity."

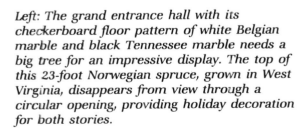

Left: The governor's tree features ornaments made by West Virginians. Two talented craftswomen crocheted and macraméd the intricate snowflake ornaments. The giant foam balls wrapped in satin ribbon and tinsel were made by the West Virginia Federation of Republican Women. The glass discs, eight inches across and weighing nearly a pound apiece, are creations by Blenko Glass, one of many fine glass manufacturers in the state.

Left: The grand entrance hall with its checkerboard floor pattern of white Belgian marble and black Tennessee marble needs a big tree for an impressive display. The top of this 23-foot Norwegian spruce, grown in West Virginia, disappears from view through a circular opening, providing holiday decoration for both stories.

Even their Christmas decorations have the stamp of made-in-West Virginia, as the photos on these pages show. And Mrs. Moore points out, "We open the house more frequently than usual during the holidays, so that the people of the state can see *their* house in its Christmas decor." And when West Virginians see the simple, meaningful symbols of Christmas, from the hearty tree grown in state soil to the delicate handmade tree ornaments, they're sure to feel that their house is in good hands.

Above left: Since guests (many from out of state) are entertained in the state dining room, it seemed appropriate that the pattern of the chair seat covers carry images pertinent to West Virginia. To develop such a design, Mrs. Moore asked a needlecrafts shop owner for help. The resulting needlepoint stitchery features a horseshoe of deep gold laurel leaves on a light background. In the center is a West Virginia monogram in shades of blue. The state flower, the rhododendron, is captured in soft pink. A contest held by the West Virginia Federation of Republican Women discovered 20 accomplished needleworkers, including one man, to execute that number of seat covers.

Left: A magazine article about a jelly bean interpretation of the White House made by President Reagan's chef inspired Ryad Salamie to surprise the Moores with a likeness of the governor's mansion in gingerbread and chocolate. (To compare, see a photo of the real mansion on page 6.) Ryad, who attended the Culinary Institute in New York before returning to his hometown of Charleston as a chef for the governor, took photos of the house to use as reference for translating the structure into sweets. The walls, roof, and grounds are sheets of gingerbread glued together with Royal Icing, which is also used liberally as decorative trim. The front walkway is paved with ginger snaps, and chocolate cups and hard candies form tiny planters. The roof (which is supported underneath by coat hangers) is covered with 99 chocolate Bavarian mint wafers.

Left: In the drawing room is an exquisite handblown glass bird, gracefully soaring over crystal waves. The artist, Robert Maretti, has been an employee of the Pilgrim Glass factory for over 25 years, and is internationally acclaimed for his one-of-a-kind works.

Below: Yet another example of West Virginia's resources, the honey-gold, luxuriously grained paneling of the library is made from butternut wood grown in the state's fruitful forestland. Over the mantel, a lush noble fir wreath is dotted with trios of red balls.

Within the capitol complex is the Cultural Center. Its gift shop is known for a well-rounded collection of works by West Virginia artists. Year-round there are quilted pieces, wonderful wood works, woven goods, heirloom dolls, stained glass, blown glass, baskets, and many other fine handcrafts, all beautifully displayed.

With a knowledgeable staff on hand to help you select unusual gifts and Christmas decorations, this is a great place for Christmas shopping. And considering the quality of materials, the fine workmanship, and the unique nature of these handmades, the prices are very reasonable.

Right: These country-look porcelain ornaments are from the Rocky Marsh Potters of Shepherdstown. The flat shapes are lightweight for tree hanging, while handpainted strokes add lots of dimension. The whimsical assortment has country favorites such as hearts, birds, and houses; Christmas symbols including stockings, candy canes, and Saint Nick; and some surprise designs—a whale, a sailboat, and a penguin.

Right: The bears in this wee family range from three-quarters inch to two inches in height, and fit in the palm of a hand. Karen Ray, the teddy bear artist from Hamlin, makes these adorable miniatures in Ultrasuede from a 17-piece pattern. Arms and legs are jointed—an amazing detail at this scale.

Above left: The lighted trees that line the drive to the capitol represent species common to the state. The building with its stately rotunda was styled after the Capitol in Washington.

Left: This nighttime illumination of the Georgian-style governor's mansion reveals the capitol in the background. It's a short walk from home to office for the governor.

Christmas with a Cajun Accent

Spanish moss drips like syrup from everything that holds still long enough in the Cajun country. At least it seems that way. When the Acadians (or Cajuns) arrived there from Canada 250 years ago, they thought the moss looked like a Spaniard's beard and called it *barbe espagnol.*

Visit south Louisiana at Christmastime now, and you'll find Spanish moss festooning porches, bannisters, and mantels the way pine boughs and magnolia leaves do elsewhere in the South. Native materials are one of the threads tying past to present for modern-day Cajuns like John and Laulie Folse. Food is another. John is owner-chef of Lafitte's Landing, a restaurant on the Mississippi River, so named because it's the legendary home of the pirate Jean Lafitte.

At John's restaurant, diners experience what he calls "local Louisiana specialties of seafood and game that are sauced with Cajunized versions of classic French sauces." Dishes include award-winning gumbo, soft-shell crab topped with crawfish and sauce Provençal, veal medallions, fillet of redfish in a meunière sauce, and Cajun fettuccine, which contains andouille (sausage) and crawfish. (John's special holiday dinner recipes start on page 90.)

Just minutes from the restaurant is the Folses' beautiful old Acadian plantation

Above: The Folse home was begun in 1854, but its builder, Andrew Gingry, died at the hands of Northern soldiers before its completion. His widow finished the house and named it Bittersweet Plantation. At the sidewalk, two pedestals hold cannonballs fired on the Gingry property during the Civil War. This house is one of two in Donaldsonville to survive the torches of Union soldiers.

Opposite: What could be more appropriate than a toque atop a chef's tree? Below the billowy white hat, natural materials such as Spanish moss and painted lotus pods fill in around ornaments the Folses have collected through the years. On the table, muscadine vines, painted pomegranates, and magnolia blossoms add color and texture to the centerpiece arrangement.

Left: Louisiana vegetation provides all the beauty and variety the Folses could need to decorate their home for the holidays. On the mantel in their dining room, drift cyprus, wild muscadine leaves, cedar branches, and Spanish moss form a true-to-life setting for this small bayou gator. Wide red velvet ribbon woven through the flora adds just the right holiday flourish.

11

home. As they move through its rooms, describing the history of the house and the area, John's speech carries subtle traces of a Cajun accent. Laulie's accent is even more elusive.

Even so, their heritage is clear. The Folses' Donaldsonville home has been in Laulie's family since her great-grandfather, a descendant of the exiled Acadians, built it over one hundred years ago. (For more on Acadian history, see page 17.)

"We found a diary that described the first restoration in 1919," John says. "There was another one after that, and we used the diary when we restored it in 1979."

The spacious house remains typically Acadian. Transom windows over doorways allow cool air to flow through the rooms. The full-length front gallery is cool in the summer, and chimneys that serve two fireplaces each, back to back, add warmth as well as old-fashioned charm in the winter. The high-pitched roofline, broken with a dormer, quickly throws off Louisiana rain, just as it cut through Canadian snow.

But the house is not only well suited to the climate, it's perfect for entertaining. "Each year we throw a big Christmas party," John says. "Laulie always fixes the house up, and we have all our friends in—lots of people." From the flash in his eye it's clear that the Folses live up to the Cajun motto "Laissez les bon temps rouler!" or "Let the good times roll!"

Above: In the Folses' living room is a painting by Cajun artist George Rodrigue. The Cajun girl's hat is echoed by mantel decorations.

Right: Here you can almost hear Santa in the Cajun Night Before Christmas urging on the alligators that pull his pirogue as he takes gifts to the bayou children. In this version, his parting words are "Merry Christmas to all 'til I saw you some mo'!"

Opposite: In the library, Rodrigue's painting of crawfishermen listening to Cajun musicians sets the tone for the room's trimmings.

Of Oaks and Fiery Tradition

In the early 1700s, a Frenchman planted 28 oaks in two rows between his home and the Mississippi River. The trees were live oaks—so named because they remain green year-round—and as they grew, they formed a vast alley all the way to the river.

Legend has it that for his daughter's wedding, the Frenchman imported large spiders from France. They wove enormous webs in the trees which were then sprinkled with gold dust and lit from behind for the evening nuptials. Of course, legends are rife in south Louisiana, and there's no reason the house in Vacherie should be left out.

By the time Jacques Télesphore Roman built a mansion on that land for his bride,

---

Inset, this page: The bonfires supposedly began so that Santa could find the Acadians after they were forced from Canada. Stacked logs form a framework that is filled with sugar cane reeds, and once lit, the flames spit and crack in the night, sending sparks darting high into the darkness.

Inset, opposite: At the appropriate moment, Santa Claus reads the Cajun Night Before Christmas with a lilting accent, a church choir performs, and Andrew Hall's Society Jazz Band of New Orleans picks up its instruments to lead guests from the house down the alley to the enormous bonfire by the river.

Left: After almost 300 years, the trees look a bit like gnarled old hands holding tufts of greenery toward the sky to catch both rain and sun. When dusk falls, luminarias light the way from the house to the river. It is under this canopy that party goers follow the jazz band to light the first bonfire of the year on the Mississippi.

Marie Thérèse Célina Josephine Pilie, the century-old trees were majestic. In 1839 Roman's house was finished, and Madame Roman named it Bon Sejour, or pleasant sojourn. As people traveling on the river saw the new plantation, however, the trees created such an impression that the mansion became known as Oak Alley.

Through the years, the mansion passed through many hands, finally falling into disrepair until Andrew and Josephine Stewart bought it in 1925 and fully restored it. Today the estate is operated through a trust set up by Josephine Stewart and administered by her grandnephew Zeb Mahew, Jr.

The house is not a museum: it is still a working sugar plantation, and the Stewarts' furnishings remain. The house is meant to be used, and it is. Each December visitors drive along the famous River Road to attend Oak Alley's annual candlelight tours and bonfire party. Regional fare is served, glasses are raised, carols and jazz waft through the night air, and in the cool evening celebrations, time seems to stand still.

Above left: Oak Alley is decorated each year with greenery gathered from the grounds and the traditional fruit, such as this apple pyramid in the dining room. A prized lace tablecloth and crystal candelabra that belonged to the Stewarts grace the Duncan Phyfe table, and a portrait of Josephine Stewart hangs over the sideboard. On the night of Oak Alley's annual bonfire party, every surface in this room is filled with Louisiana treats such as seafood gumbo, crab dip, baked oysters, jambalaya, and crawfish en croute.

Left: This second story bedroom faces down the alley of oaks that gives the plantation its name. This room, like many others in the house, received fresh draperies and other furnishings when Oak Alley was used for the television remake of The Long Hot Summer.

Joyeux Noël from the Acadian Village

The time was the mid-18th century. Emmeline LaBiche, a young Acadian, arrived in south Louisiana after the British forced her people from their adopted homeland of Nova Scotia and New Brunswick. Emmeline was separated not only from her family and friends, but also from her betrothed. As she boarded the ship, she vowed to wait for him, and wait she did—for the rest of her life.

Tragic true stories like this one formed the basis for Longfellow's famous poem "Evangeline." For the Acadians, the struggle to survive was a hard one. Most of the exiles drifted to the other French-speaking territory on this continent—south Louisiana—and worked to rebuild their lives. But the memory of that period helped shape a culture that, even with the intrusion of the twentieth century, is one of the most individual in the country. It's a culture that is preserved at the Acadian Village, a folk life museum in Lafayette, Louisiana.

At the Acadian Village, visitors can experience Cajun village life as it was a century ago. Period homes have been moved to a man-made bayou and refurbished. Old materials were used to build a general store, chapel, and blacksmith shop, and the village sits in 10 acres of woods. It was in just such a setting that these immigrants from northern France lived their simple life of fishing, trapping, and farming. But the Cajuns are best known for their fondness for music and dancing, good food, and good times.

During the Christmas season, their fun-loving streak was tempered by their religious devotion. Christmas itself was a time for quiet worship. The Cajuns attended midnight mass, enjoyed a good meal, and the children received fruit given to them, not by Santa Claus, but by *l'enfant Jesus*. The big celebration came at New Year's when the Cajuns exchanged their gifts (usually

Top: This chapel, built with 200-year-old Louisiana longleaf pine, is a replica of an 1850 Cajun chapel.

Above: Each December, the Lafayette Junior League stages "Christmas Comes Alive" to fund its many worthwhile community projects.

handmade), prepared lavish feasts, and visited family and friends.

Today, Christmas at the Acadian Village is spectacular. For nine days every year, the village dons Christmas finery to serve as a fund-raising project of the Lafayette Junior League. Lights outline the bayou and walkways, working animations bring a wonderland quality to the old homes, and Santa and his elves welcome the many visitors.

Over this magical scene towers a 35-foot light tree. And each year thousands of visitors stroll through the village while the tree casts flickering reflections in the bayou, shifting colors in the winter night.

Chinqua-Penn Plantation: Eclectic Elegance

Tucked away among the tobacco fields and dairy farms of Rockingham County, North Carolina, is Chinqua-Penn Plantation House. For forty years it was the home of tobacco magnate Thomas Jefferson Penn and his wife, Beatrice Schoellkopf Penn. The Penns named the house after the chinquapin bushes found in abundance on the grounds, altering the spelling of the bush to incorporate their own name. Jeff and Betsy Penn traveled the world in search of the priceless furniture, tapestries, and religious icons which fill their Shangri-la.

The elaborate, antique furniture and museum-quality tapestries throughout the house are a testament to the spirit of the

Above: The Florentine mantel in the main living room dates back to the Renaissance and is draped with a garland and wreath of pine, holly, and holly berries. The 17th-century tapestry over the mantel depicts Moses receiving the Ten Commandments. It is a product of the Beauvais factory in France, which at one time catered to the French nobility. Gracing the mantel is a 16th-century Spanish Madonna with a sterling silver halo. Adoration figures from the same period surround the Madonna.

Above: Situated on the crest of a knoll, Chinqua-Penn was built in a Y-shape to capture the maximum amount of sunlight and to provide the best air circulation. The twenty-seven room house is built of native North Carolina stone and oak logs felled on the site.

Opposite: Hand-painted, exposed beams accentuate the 65-foot ceiling in the main living room. The light fixtures in this immense room are Chinese temple lanterns.

Above: A wall of windows overlooking the rose garden gives the breakfast room its airiness. While in Rome, the Penns were so impressed by an Italian artist that they invited him to live at Chinqua-Penn while he painted the panels in the breakfast room.

Right: Located in Mrs. Penn's sitting room is this antique Italian mantel. Blue-and-ivory tiles that show artisans at their craft outline the front of the mantel, and an 18th-century painted panel hangs above it. This room was Mrs. Penn's favorite, and her collection of fans, statues, and religious icons is displayed here.

individualists who responded so energetically to the objets d'art they saw all over the world. By bringing this bounty home, the Penns made it possible for thousands to savor the beauty and history of this diverse collection and experience the same joy of discovery.

The Penns' most consistent idea when collecting for and decorating the house was the avoidance of one certain period or style. But continuity runs through the decor of Chinqua-Penn in the form of good humor, enthusiasm, and a true appreciation for skillful craftsmanship. In this eclectic approach to decorating, the Penns were ahead of their time.

The Penns built and furnished Chinqua-Penn for their own purpose and pleasure, yet never isolated the house or themselves from the community. Farm meetings as well as fundraisers were held at Chinqua-Penn.

Above: The stone floor in the Mud Room made it possible for the Penns and their guests to relax and refresh themselves while still wearing their muddy riding boots. Over the mantel is a fresco from Greece. A rare collection of 16th- and 17th-century spurs and bits hangs on the right wall. Russia, China, and Africa are some of the exotic lands represented by the furnishings in this room.

Following Mrs. Penn's death in 1965, the house and grounds were given to the University of North Carolina (UNC). Today, UNC at Greensboro is caretaker of the house and grounds, while North Carolina State University operates the 900 acres that were designated for use in tobacco research and as a 4-H camp. Chinqua-Penn is open for public tours from March 1 through the third Sunday in December.

The Christmas season at Chinqua-Penn begins after Thanksgiving, when the house is decorated with garlands and wreaths made from materials grown on the grounds. All poinsettias used in the house come from the greenhouse, including the pink poinsettias which are cultivated in honor of Betsy Penn's favorite color. Candlelight tours are scheduled for two special nights during the Christmas season. One thousand luminarias, assembled by the greenhouse staff, line the drive and the front of the house. Local choirs and handbell groups fill the main living room with the sound of Christmas carols for the evening visitors. During breaks in the music program, visitors and performers are treated to hot spiced tea and cookies.

Above: One thousand luminarias surround the house and line the drive, lighting the way to Chinqua-Penn during the evening tours.

Above: The delicate music of the Kirkringers from Leaksville United Methodist Church in Eden, North Carolina, evokes an ethereal splendor as the music of their handbells floats through the main living room.

Right: Serenade, a ladies' singing group from Reidsville, North Carolina, entertains visitors with Christmas carols in the main living room during the delightful evening tours at Chinqua-Penn.

Shakertown: A World Apart

Shakertown at Pleasant Hill, 25 miles southwest of Lexington, Kentucky, offers Winter Weekends (from late December into March) that may be just the kind of vacation you need after the hectic holidays. This village was built between 1809 and 1855 by the Shakers, a religious sect known for praying themselves into a frenzied dance, shaking their bodies wildly to get rid of evil spirits. In 1823 Shakers lived here, but the society dwindled in the latter half of the 1800s, and became inactive in 1910. Village restoration began in 1966.

A Shaker's life was worship and work, as the "hands to work, hearts to God" philosophy professed. As millenarians, they believed in Christ's second coming (as a

Above: The four-story Centre Family Dwelling has two entrance doors, double stairs, and wide common halls which allowed for separation of the sexes.

woman) within a thousand years. They practiced confession of sins, communal ownership, celibacy, and withdrawal from the world, except for necessary trade. (The Shaker seed industry was widely known.) Ahead of their time, Shakers upheld equality of the sexes and races.

At Shakertown, don't expect to see decorations, Christmas or otherwise. Shaker belief in simplicity and utility left no room for embellishment. (Individual artists could not even sign their work.) But Shaker architecture, furnishings, and household accessories were distinctly beautiful—unadorned, yet extraordinarily artful, with graceful lines, functional purity, and durability. As a logical outgrowth of their belief in conservation of resources, they designed every tool to expedite work, leaving more time and energy for prayer. Their inventions include the circular saw, washing machine, and metal pen point.

If you decide to be a Winter Weekend guest, you'll sleep in private quarters in an original building, furnished with some of Pleasant Hill's 2,500-piece collection of Shaker furniture and tools. (Accommodations are available for families and groups, as well.) You'll be served Shaker-style country cooking at communal tables. At these meals, you can compare impressions with fellow visitors, unlike earlier days when Shaker men and women ate separately and silently to save time. Around the village, you can watch quilters, spinners, weavers, cabinet makers, and broom makers at work. (The flat broom was another Shaker creation.) And coopers demonstrate the shaping of the famed Shaker wood boxes.

On a visit to Shakertown, you're sure to admire the handiwork and inventiveness of these dedicated people, and acquire a new appreciation for some of today's conveniences, compliments of Shaker ingenuity. And in this quiet, simple setting, you'll gain insight into a lifestyle very different from what most of us live today. Anticipate a visit to Shakertown as an opportunity to learn and to refresh yourself for the year ahead.

Decorating for the Holidays

Deck the halls, the doors, the windows, and the tabletops. Place holiday decorations in every room so that festive touches will be everywhere you look. Or trim the tree with a carefully selected theme, match that look at the mantel, and then carry it to your dining room centerpiece. Or set out a single beloved decoration, and let that lone symbol say it all, simply and sincerely.

There are many ways to go about decorating for the holidays. Some people collect an assortment of decorations and scatter them throughout the house, rejoicing in the fond memories that each object summons. Some prefer a more cohesive theme, coordinated through color, motif, and style, and delight in that one-of-a-kind, one-time-only creation. Others like to keep it simple, opting for a few special elements.

However you choose to decorate, we hope the images on the following pages will inspire you. Among the possibilities presented here, you'll find a fresh, flowery influence—on the tree, on the table, around the house—decorations that rely on nature's delicate marvels.

There are also decorations to make that will take your loving time and last for years, like the whitework stocking or the embroidered angel ornaments. And there are trimmings that will take only a few minutes to accomplish, like the tree swathed in gold lamé, or the little wreaths made of embroidery floss. These are just a few of the offerings to get you started on this year's celebration and tomorrow's memories.

The Flowering of Christmas

From the exotic flowers that wondrously blossom on these evergreen trees, to artful arrangements thoughtfully situated around the house or serving graciously as centerpieces on the following pages, there seems to be a trend toward the flowering of Christmas. A luxurious indulgence, especially in midwinter, fresh and fragrant flowers make for a heady holiday experience.

The disadvantage to flowers as tree trims, of course, is their passing beauty. Yet, their loveliness may be worth the brief display, their fragile and transient nature inspiring an even deeper appreciation than a more lasting ornament.

The flowers used here and on the tree on the following page should last from three days (the airy orchid cymbidiums), to almost two weeks (the Hawaiian anthuriums), when placed in florist's vials. The bird-of-paradise flowers have thick stems that will not fit into a vial, but even so, they may last up to a week. (Keeping your house fairly cool will also prolong freshness.)

These fancy flowers are rather expensive. But there are many less expensive alternatives that would work very well on the tree, such as camellias, carnations, chrysanthemums, or lilies. Consult your florist. He can

Opposite and above right: Lavished with green cymbidiums (orchids), this tree sets the stage for a very special holiday occasion. Though rather expensive, cymbidiums make one of the most elegant tree trims imaginable. And even after the delicate blooms are gone, shimmering white lights and scallops of velvety peach ribbon will make the tree attractive.

tell you what flowers are available and the current prices. (He may even be able to offer you good deals on flowers with broken stems.) Another way to reduce cost is to decorate a small tabletop tree instead of a larger one.

Begin by decorating your tree so that it will be pretty with or without the flowers. That way you can trim it in advance and time the addition of blossoms to coincide with your entertainment schedule. Then as flowers fade, you can pull them out, and the tree will still be beautifully dressed.

Left and above: Vivid bird-of-paradise flowers and white anthuriums (a long-lasting choice) adorn this tree with tropical vitality. Other trims include baby's breath, brass shells, strands of pearls, dangling crystal prisms, and silver and white balls.

Make Flowers the Center of Attention

When friends gather around the table to share a holiday meal, an unusual centerpiece can start conversation flowing merrily along. Just as a winding path through the woods beckons you to explore, a centerpiece of uncommon flowers and other natural materials invites you to come closer, to breathe the refreshing fragrance and relish the delicate beauty. And once enticed by sight and scent, your guests may even engage in a name-that-plant contest.

In creating a centerpiece for a sit-down dinner, be careful that the height of the arrangement does not interfere with diners' views across the table. A too-tall centerpiece may hamper conversation, especially at a small dining table with only a few people seated around it. A long, low-to-the-table arrangement or one or more medium-height arrangements will work nicely.

But if you're serving refreshments from a buffet or other serving area, that's the time for a spectacular dining room table display. Not only will it transform the large surface of your dining table into an attractive decoration for the occasion, it will encourage the flow of people, inviting guests to circle about the floral showcase.

Right: This centerpiece has oriental flair. Clear plastic rods, rooted in florist's foam, are dramatically vertical, and whitewashed bamboo draws strong horizontal lines. On the mirror are white spray-painted cones and pods, white anthuriums, Ming moss, and Ming fern. Star-of-Bethlehem, allium, and dendrobium sprout from this mass. A nest, springing from a platform of florist's foam caged in wire mesh, repeats the same materials. Four more rods rise from here to the top to support another nest.

Above: A random array of pink and red anthuriums, gerbera daisies, variegated holly, star-of-Bethlehem, Queen Anne's lace, and white lilies make an open and airy crown to this centerpiece. To anchor the arrangement, fresh fruit—apples, grapes, and pears— overflow a silver pedestal bowl. Floating on a mirror and encircled by tall tapers, the composition has an elegant and formal tone.

Right: This arrangement is a naturalistic design, a popular European approach to flower arranging. Asian lilies, white protea, white freesia, bouvardia, and flowering quince emerge from undergrowth of boxwood, magnolia leaves, sweet pea and ivy vines, spruce, and leatherleaf fern to suggest the abundant tropical vegetation one might expect on the fertile banks of a jungle stream.

Singular Sensations

During the holidays, there may be a place in your home that you would like to dress up, where typical Christmas decorations would seem incongruous. Perhaps you just can't reconcile yourself to bringing holiday colors, motifs, and materials into a carefully planned decorating scheme, and desire a tribute to the season that exactly suits your room. Fresh flowers suit almost any location and coordinate with all styles. At the same time, through fragrance, texture, and color, they quietly call for attention, lending a fresh new look to everyday surroundings.

Creating a floral arrangement can be a stress-relieving activity during the hectic holidays, a time to yourself to create a thing of beauty. Gather materials from your yard or the woods, and make a trip to your florist. (You might call first to see what he has available and to plan your design.) Consider what size of arrangement will best suit the location, and even take approximate measurements—a too-small display may look almost pitiful in an overwhelming situation, and an oversized one could be in the way and get knocked over.

If your problem is having too little time and too few decorations for an upcoming party, let your florist do the arrangement for you. Just give him an idea of where you want to use the arrangement with regard to color and scale.

Left: An arrangement of rubrum lilies, fir boughs, and branches berried with tiny foam balls overspreads and draws attention to this unusually knobbed and hinged wooden chest.

Opposite: These twin mantel arrangements are light and airy, in keeping with a tree of graceful angels. White lilies and carnations, mingled with fragrant eucalyptus and corkscrew willow branches, seem to float in midair in large glass vases.

Above: In this small, yet distinctive, arrangement, palmetto palm fronds form a definitive backdrop, with pine intermittently interrupting the outline. Dried yarrow provides a lovely yellow color, crab apples add red, and the yellow-and-green speckled leaves of aucuba unify the materials.

Opposite: Against the warmth of red-brown paneling and a shiny brass chest, this arrangement is a rich textural treat. Graceful stems of cymbidium orchids arch outward from a cluster of cedar sprays. Bare branches trace extending lines above and to the sides of the arrangement, suggesting an even larger scale. Pears, apples, and limes peek out from the base.

Nature's Gold

Dried to honey gold and intermingled with living luxuriance, this bounty from nature furnishes an elegance appropriate to the setting. The rich glow of dried flowers and berries creates a stunning contrast to the vibrant red and green surrounding it.

Opposite, the Queen Anne-style melodeon (a small reed organ) is crowned with an arrangement featuring lustrous golden allium and snowflake hydrangea set among Chinese tallow, holly berries, pine and noble fir branches, and pinecones. Many of the same materials are carried upward, where green branches and gold flowers crest the oval mirror.

Shimmering from a marble tabletop, the Fraser fir, below, is ornamented with little more than golden blossoms. Bows and glass balls supply red accents amidst dried snowflake hydrangea, allium, holly berries, and roses from Holland.

On the mantel at left, florist's foam secures a flounce of gorse and pine branches, asparagus fern fronds, poinsettias, and dried snowflake hydrangea and allium. Beneath it, a swell of poinsettias overflows the fireplace and is flanked by two vine swans embellished with snowflake hydrangea and Spanish moss.

38

Silvery Bell Wreath

Silver bells and swirls of shiny silver ribbon transform a cleverly wrought vine bell into an elegant door decoration.

Bells lilt along the sides of the wreath, dangle airily in its center, and masquerade as a clapper beneath the fluffy silver bow. Tucked in a corner of the wreath, a tiny white bird looks ready to add its song to the tinkling of the bells.

Fashion this wreath from fresh-cut vines, spray with white paint, and then freely deck it with ribbon and bell flourishes. Set against a richly colored door, as shown here, this bell-shaped wreath is a lovely and unusual holiday statement.

Materials:
- **20″ square of ½″ plywood**
- **24 (3″) nails**
- **fresh-cut vines (cut before frost)**
- **white spray paint**
- **10 yards each size (1½″-wide, ¼″-wide, ⅛″-wide) silver satin ribbon**
- **22 yards (³⁄₁₆″-wide) silver metallic curling ribbon**
- **craft glue**
- **11 (1″-wide) silver plastic bells**
- **2 (1¾″-wide) silver plastic bells**
- **small white bird**

Create a pattern for a bell 15″ high and 15″ at bottom by drawing half of the shape and reversing it for a symmetrical outline. Following Diagram 1, transfer bell pattern to wood and drive nails ¼″ into wood to outline bell. Wrap vines around the bell form, twisting and weaving to hold the vines together. Always weave vine ends under other vines, and begin each new vine at a different spot on the wreath.

When form is full, allow vines to dry several days. Remove wreath from form and add more vines until all points on wreath measure 8″ around. Let wreath dry for several more days.

Spray several coats of paint on each side of wreath. Let dry between coats.

To make ribbon bow: following Diagrams 2, 3, and 4, loop 1½″-wide silver ribbon in several 8″ circles, fold in half, notch on both sides at center, and tie tightly with about 10″ of the ⅛″-wide ribbon. Pull the loops out, and twist to shape a bow. Tie to the bottom of the wreath with ends of narrow ribbon and trim the excess. Cut loose ends of wide ribbon at an angle or in a V.

Cut lengths of the different widths of ribbon and drape loosely around wreath, gluing to vines in several places. Use narrower widths of ribbon to tie bells and bird onto wreath as shown in photo.

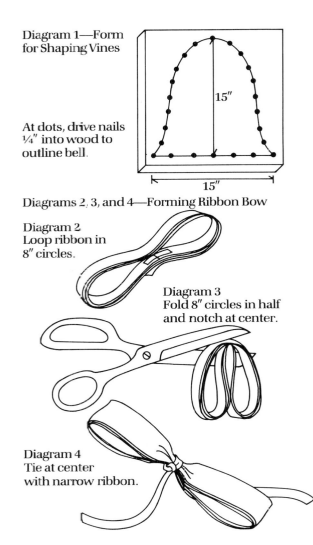

Diagram 1—Form for Shaping Vines

At dots, drive nails ¼″ into wood to outline bell.

15″

15″

Diagrams 2, 3, and 4—Forming Ribbon Bow

Diagram 2
Loop ribbon in 8″ circles.

Diagram 3
Fold 8″ circles in half and notch at center.

Diagram 4
Tie at center with narrow ribbon.

A Christmas Composition

Voices raised in carols touch memories deep within all of us. The songs of the season underscore the reverence of Christmas and provide much of its excitement. Whether music plays a major role in your life, or you simply enjoy its special beauty during the holidays, consider a musical theme when you deck the halls this year.

Start by assembling the old saxophone, dusting off the piano, or polishing the guitar. Any instruments you have around the house can make one-of-a-kind decorations. The inclusion of a simple bow and careful placement of an ornament might be just the touches you need.

If there isn't a horn in your attic, garage sales are a good bet for finding inexpensive instruments suitable for decorations. Holiday shops, flea markets, antique shops, and importer's stores carry both real and mock instruments that are reasonable in price.

Try filling an opened instrument case with an abundance of dried flowers. Place it near a doorway, beside a fireplace, or between candles on a chest.

As you can see in many of the photos on these pages, printed music seems both warm and familiar. Find music, or paper

Left: To make the ornaments shown on this tree, transfer the patterns on pages 138 and 139 to two-sided musical paper, and cut them out with a craft knife. Experiment with other designs, such as quilt motifs, ornaments you already have, and any other silhouettes that suit your decor. Punch a hole in the top of each ornament, and run a length of thin gold cord through it for a hanger. Then try nestling the ornaments in an ample green wreath, attaching them to the top of a package—even suspending them from a branch tree in a foyer or breakfast nook.

40

Above: Invite carolers in to warm up. They'll be right at home in a room decorated to celebrate the music of the season. Caroling dates back to the old English practice of going from house to house wassailing, or toasting "wes hál"—be well! Long-treasured songs help maintain that tie to the past.

Left: On the piano, a modified French horn serves as a candle holder and is trimmed with pine, holly, and a piece of music. A bit of careful singeing around the edges of the paper, plus accordion folding, renders it "antiqued" and ready for inclusion in an arrangement such as this one. Then bright red ribbon ties the composition together and furnishes the needed spark of color.

41

with a musical design, and use it as gift wrap for small presents. Then turn a grouping of them into a centerpiece. Accordionfolded, the paper makes a sculptural replacement for the traditional bow on a package. Or use a heavy paper, and make place cards and invitations for a party.

The photos and descriptions on these pages suggest other ways to create decorative musical arrangements.

Right: Two brass horns, tucked behind an ornamental violin, become the focal point of an arrangement over this fireplace. Pine, cedar, variegated holly, and eucalyptus form a lavish blanket behind the instruments. Sea grape leaves lead the eye in a gentle S curve through the exquisite assemblage, and pheasant feathers and curly willow vines dramatically twist and stretch outward. Dried materials repeat the colors of the feathers and vines while adding mass to the design. And vibrant, contrasting hues come from roses, lilies, and rich red ribbon. On the floor, a grouping of horns carries the theme to the hearth, and a basket of Jingle Bell poinsettias injects an extra splash of red.

Right: An asymmetrical spray adorns this ornate music stand without interfering with its function. Focused by a starlike white lily, the free-form cluster repeats the greenery and ribbon used elsewhere in the room. Spanish moss fills in where needed to hide glimpses of the foam holding the spray.

Opposite: Lush and overflowing, greenery centered with a French horn crowns this armoire. Florist's foam taped into three oblong containers forms the base for magnolia leaves, pine, cedar, variegated holly, elaeagnus, red roses, white tulips, and pheasant feathers. A profusion of red ribbon blooms in bunches and flows in and out among the natural elements.

This arrangement, scaled to fit, would be striking on a library table, sideboard, or mantel. Make sure you protect wood surfaces with a layer of foil or plastic.

Sweet Melody with Each Hello

Let a trilling cascade of notes help you welcome holiday visitors each time you open your door. This unusual harp makes an entertaining holiday decoration that will continue to brighten each passage, long after the season has ended.

Recruit a skillful hand to cut and assemble the four pieces that make up the harp body; then finish it to blend with any decor. For Christmas cheer, attach a fluffy, bright red bow and a pouch of potpourri, or surround the harp with ornament-sprinkled greenery. If the strings loosen with time, just tighten them with a screwdriver to keep the melody sweet.

Materials:
patterns on page 139
10″ (1″ x 12″) wood
6″ square (⅛″-thick) wood
jigsaw
router with ¼″ round-over bit
½″ #8 wire brads
sandpaper
6″ square (⅜″-thick) wood
wood glue
wood clamps
drill with 1/16″ and 3/16″ bits
8 (1¼″) #8 brass screws
small-diameter musical instrument
  string
3 (¾″) wooden balls or beads
monofilament fishing line
round toothpicks
tung oil with varnish
fine steel wool

Cut a 10″ circle from the 1″ x 12″ and a 6″ circle from ⅛″ wood. Draw a 4″ circle slightly off center on the 10″ circle, and cut out. With router, round the inside edge of the 4″ hole and outside edge of the 10″ circle. Position the 6″ circle on the back of the 10″ circle, covering the 4″ hole, to create the sound chamber. Use wire brads to tack it in place. Lightly sand.

Transfer patterns for the 2 top pieces to ⅜″ wood. Cut out and sand. Position piece A on harp as shown in photo. Secure with glue, and clamp in place.

Using a 1/16″ bit and following the pattern, drill 3 holes through piece B to suspend the beads. Position piece B on piece A, as indicated on the pattern. Use a 3/16″ bit to pilot-drill holes for the #8 screws through pieces B and A and ½″ into the harp. Measure and tape bit to avoid drilling too far. Screw the pieces together.

Following photo, mark positions for screws that hold strings on both sides of sound hole. Make sure rows are parallel and screws are spaced about ⅛″ from sound hole. Start all 6 screws into wood. Cut musical instrument string into 3 pieces, each 9″ long. On one side of the sound hole, tie a piece of string in a knot around the top screw. Tighten the screw, stretch string tightly across to other side, and wrap it around opposite screw. Tighten screw, checking string tension for desired sound. Trim any excess string. Repeat for remaining 2 strings.

Drill a 1/16″ hole through center of each wooden bead. Cut a piece of fishing line 6″ long. Drip a small amount of glue into the hole of a bead, thread the line into the hole, and wedge it with a round toothpick. Break and sand off the protruding piece of toothpick. Repeat for the other 2 beads.

Thread one of the lines with a bead on it into the left-hand hole in piece B. Adjust the length of the line so that the bead strikes the top string. Wedge in with glue and a round toothpick, as above. Repeat process, with center bead striking center string and right bead striking bottom string.

Use fine sandpaper to smooth any remaining rough spots on harp. Apply a coat of tung oil with varnish, allow it to dry thoroughly, and smooth with fine steel wool. Repeat process to apply 2 or 3 coats, as desired.

Whitework: Understated Elegance

Snow-white doves and frosty holly with pearly berries—these graceful embroidered images come alive on a lovely heirloom stocking. The soft contrast of white thread to beige linen emphasizes each stitch. And the subtle play of light and shadow on the contoured stitchery suggests surprising depth, especially in the bird's feathers.

Materials:
   pattern and diagrams on page 140
   ½ yard (36″-wide) ecru linen or
      linen-like fabric
   10 skeins white embroidery floss
   8 yards (size 5) white perle cotton
   ⅓ yard (36″-wide) lightweight web
      interfacing (for lining)
   Fray Check
   1 yard (⅛″-wide) white ribbon
   1⅔ yards (⅝″-wide) white edging

Note: Finished size is 14″ long.

Transfer stocking pattern and design to 14″ x 18″ piece of linen. (Do not cut out.) Follow pattern instructions to embroider. Diagrams are given for less common stitches. Block completed stitchery.

Cut out embroidered stocking front. Cut out stocking back from linen and 2 lining pieces from interfacing. With right sides facing, pin and baste stocking front to back. Machine-stitch sides and bottom. Trim seams, clip curves, and apply Fray Check to clipped edges. Turn and press. Fold raw edges at top ½″ to inside and press. Stitch a 10″ ribbon loop hanger to right top corner.

Pin and machine-stitch lining pieces together, except at top. Do not turn. Slip lining into stocking. With raw edges of linen beneath lining, hand-stitch lining to folded top edge of stocking.

Hand-stitch white edging all around stocking. (If necessary, trim off the base of edging to make it more flexible.) Stitch a white ribbon bow to hanger.

Variations on an Angelic Theme

Gold trumpets herald the arrival of this airy angelic pair, brilliantly presented in white on white, and adorned with gold. Subtle differences in the embroidery thread allow these angels to shine in separate, but equally resplendent, lights.

Rayon thread provides a shiny luster in the stitches of the angel on the left, while cotton floss gives a subdued delicacy to the stitches of the angel on the right. White and gold beads accent the details of their robes and lend extra sparkle to the glowing halos. Use the stitches shown here, or experiment with your own favorites. Either way the results will be extraordinary.

Materials (for each angel):
  patterns and chart on page 144
  7″ x 10″ piece medium-weight white
    fabric
  embroidery hoop
  millinery needles
  embroidery floss or rayon thread
    (see chart)
  gold metallic thread
  gold seed beads
  pearlized white seed beads
  ½ yard iron-on interfacing
  Fray Check

Transfer design to fabric. To prevent fabric from puckering, place in embroidery hoop. Work design according to chart. (Because ornaments will be fused to a backing, secure thread ends with small backstitches to avoid knots on back of fabric.)

When work is finished, iron to fuse interfacing to wrong side of fabric. Add several layers of interfacing to create a stiff backing. Turn ornament over and apply Fray Check outside the stem stitches that outline each angel. Let dry and trim away excess fabric around ornament, cutting as close to stitching as possible.

Tucked Away for a Merry Day

The ornaments, gifts, and gift boxes shown here have two things in common. They're white, and they feature tucking. Tucking is simply small folds, stitched in place and pressed flat. Yet thanks to repetition and variations in the size and direction of the tucks, it looks intricate.

A versatile embellishment, tucking is dear on a baby's gown, polished on a woman's tailored blouse, and sophisticated on a man's dress shirt. Here, tucked house ornaments are charming personalized gifts. (Give them to yourself as heirloom reminders of happy Christmases in houses past.) A fringed woolen scarf, patterned with tucking, is a stylish practical gift. And folded paper, covering boxes you'll want to use again and again, mocks the fabric tucking.

Although you can tuck solid fabrics in any color, and also many print fabrics, these projects are all white. That's because white ornaments and boxes stand out like snow against the dark green of a Christmas tree. And a white scarf, given as a gift, will fit into any wardrobe.

SCARF

Materials (for up to 3 scarves):
 diagram on page 143
 1⅔ yards (36"-wide) lightweight 100% wool (white or desired color)
 matching thread

Note: You can make a scarf from less yardage by seaming it in the middle, but a continuous length of fabric is preferable.

Cut an 11½" x 60" piece of fabric. On short sides, stitch 2" from edges and pull threads to fringe. To hem long sides, fold under ⅛". Fold under ⅛" again and machine-stitch close to edge of fold.

To tuck, measure 1½" from fringe stitching, fold fabric over ⅜" toward fringe, press, and stitch (see Diagram on page 143). Measuring ⅜" between tucks, make 2 more ⅜" tucks as before. Next, measure 3¾" from last seam, and make five ⅜" tucks, ⅜" apart. Repeat for other end.

To finish fringe, group threads every ⅜" along the edge, and tie these groupings in knots 1" from the ends.

GIFT BOXES

Materials:
 white wrapping paper
 lidded boxes
 craft glue
 transparent tape
 ribbon

Cover bottom of box with paper, wrapping over sides to inside of box. Glue paper to inside of box and trim away excess paper. For lid, fold paper in desired tucking pattern. (To achieve desired effect, experiment with kraft paper or even newspaper, varying size and direction of folds.) Tape folds in place from back. Allowing excess paper to fold inside, cover lid with tucked paper. Add ribbon bows as desired.

HOUSE ORNAMENTS

Materials:
   patterns and diagram on page 143
   **unbleached muslin (for tucked house
      shape)**
   scraps of white fabric
   matching thread
   lace and other decorative trims
   gold metallic thread
   10″ cream ribbon

Trace pattern on paper, or draw your own. Draw windows, doors, house numbers, or other details. Draw lines indicating direction and size of tucks (see Diagram). (Horizontal tucking gives the impression of a wooden frame house. For the look of brick, stitch vertically over horizontal tucking.)

To determine how much fabric is needed for the ornament front: for width, measure across the house pattern. For the length, double the measurement of a single tuck, multiply by the desired number of tucks, add the height of the house (or, if using a textured fabric for the roof, measure from the bottom of the house to the roofline). Tuck the entire piece of fabric. Transfer pattern including details. Cut out along outline.

For window, cut an opening ⅛″ inside pattern lines. Clip to corners; turn under ⅛″. Cut a piece of muslin ¼″ larger all around than window. Hand-stitch lines for panes. Place muslin behind opening; if desired, slip lace for curtain between window piece and house front. Stitch window in place.

For doors, cut out a piece of muslin, or other textured fabric, ⅛″ larger all around than door. Stitch details on door. Turn under edges ⅛″, and stitch door in place.

Machine- or hand-stitch other details, as desired. Stitch the house numbers and doorknobs with gold metallic thread.

For back of ornament, cut house shape from muslin. For a hanger, fold ribbon in half and insert fold between house front and back (right sides facing). Sew front and back together, leaving bottom open. Turn, stuff ornament, and stitch opening closed.

A Golden Spiral for the Tree

For visual impact, drape a tree in fabric. This creates a bold, dramatic, and sophisticated statement, and with little effort required. You simply begin at the top of the tree, by securing a continuous length of fabric with ribbon or florist's wire. Then wrap fabric around the tree in a downward spiral, resting it on limbs for support.

Gold lamé swirls about the tree shown here. Silk flowers, clusters of natural materials, floating cherubs, and long ribbon streamers of gold, peach, and burgundy add the finishing touch.

Besides lamé, other good choices for fabric would be net, lace, or sheer, gauzy materials. Or for a country-style tree, use red-and-white gingham. To estimate the amount of fabric needed to drape your tree, wrap string where you will want fabric; then measure the string for yardage. The width of the fabric can vary from a foot to a yard, depending on the weight (the lighter the fabric, the wider you can go).

Eyelet and Plaid: A Pretty Set

Begin an old-fashioned Christmas with a tree skirt made from creamy eyelet fabric, and decorated with red-and-green plaid Christmas trees, which you hand-appliqué and quilt. A border of eyelet trim encircles the plaid forest for a tree skirt so pretty that you'll think twice before covering it with presents. Then, repeat this motif at your Christmas table. Plaid Christmas trees serve as napkin holders when appliquéd to pre-quilted place mats.

Place Mats

Materials:
> pattern on page 142
> ⅓ yard (45"-wide) red-and-green plaid fabric
> 4 ecru pre-quilted place mats
> ¾ yard (¼"-wide) red satin ribbon

Transfer tree pattern to plaid fabric and cut out 8 trees. Place 2 tree cutouts right sides facing, and stitch around outer edge, leaving an opening for turning. Clip corners, turn, and stitch opening closed.

Position a tree on the left side of each place mat and appliqué the bottom half of the tree to the mat, leaving the top half of the tree open for the napkin. Cut ribbon into 4 equal lengths and tie in bows. Tack one bow to the base of each tree.

Tree Skirt

Materials:
> pattern on page 142
> 1¼ yards (45"-wide) ecru eyelet fabric
> 1¼ yards (45"-wide) ecru fabric (for backing)
> 1¼ yards (45"-wide) batting
> ½ yard red-and-green plaid fabric
> green thread
> 4¼ yards (1"-wide) ruffled ecru eyelet trim
> ecru thread (for quilting)
> 4 yards (¼"-wide) red satin ribbon

Cut a 45" circle from eyelet fabric, backing, and batting. On wrong side of eyelet fabric, draw a line from edge of fabric to the center, and mark a 6½" circle. (Do not cut out.)

Transfer tree pattern to plaid fabric and cut out 16 trees. Space trees evenly around the outer edge of the right side of the eyelet fabric, 2½" from the bottom edge of the fabric. Pin trees in place and appliqué them to the tree skirt by turning the edges under ⅛" and blind-stitching to the eyelet fabric. With right sides facing, align the straight edge of the trim with the raw edge of the eyelet fabric (scalloped edge of trim towards center), and stitch.

Place eyelet fabric on top of backing, right sides facing, and place batting on the bottom. Pin layers together. Cut center back line to center point of circle, and cut out center circle as marked. Starting at the center back line, and leaving an opening for turning, stitch all 3 layers together, with a ¼" seam. (Follow stitching line made by attaching eyelet edging and tuck in ends of trim at center back corners.) Clip all corners, turn, and stitch opening closed. Iron.

Place the tree skirt on a flat surface eyelet side up. Quilt around each tree with a running stitch. To conceal a knot, pull knot through the backing and into the batting. To finish quilting, make a single backstitch and cut the thread. Tie 16 bows from the red ribbon and tack one bow at the center base of each tree.

A Flossy Wreath

Here the popular grapevine wreath is reinterpreted in miniature, with embroidery floss wrapped in a circle. Applied to cards and packages, it's an ingenious topping that will charm the recipient. It's also delightfully easy to accomplish.

For each wreath, you'll need two shades of floss, one yard of each. Wrap lengths around and around in a circle, twisting as you wrap. (For the wreath size shown here, floss was wrapped around four fingers.)

Lay circle of floss flat and apply a line of craft glue to side facing up. Pick up floss wreath carefully, turn over, and position on desired surface. Let dry in place. If ends show, tuck into wreath. Tie a bow from narrow ribbon, and glue at top or bottom of wreath. Twist streamers and secure ribbon to surface with a tiny dot of glue.

Serve Up Good Wishes

Serve up good wishes as well as good cheer during your holiday hostessing, with Christmas greetings incorporated into a serving tray. Cross-stitched in bright red and green, with gold filigree, the Aida cloth is mounted on cardboard and placed beneath a glass top. This ensures that your handiwork will be protected when you offer guests Christmas confections and libations.

Materials:
   chart and color key on page 145
   20-count Aida cloth
   embroidery floss (see color chart)
   gold metallic thread
   9″ x 12″ purchased serving tray kit

Work design on Aida cloth, according to charts. Block design, center on cardboard backing, and attach. Put tray together according to directions and place glass piece over design.

Merry Christmas Critters

Christmas in some parts of the country may mean sleigh bells and snow. But here, creatures of the Southern woods and shore are decked out for the holidays. Make these cheery critters, diverse in technique and design, to add to your collection of ornaments. (Instructions on following page.)

Give the raccoon's body a fuzzy, furry appearance with Persian yarn. Then create contrast with delicate embroidered stitches of shiny floss to outline and highlight the different elements of the ornament. Redbirds, cross-stitched and outlined with beads, are ready to nest in your tree or table arrangements. And needlepointed atop pier-post perches is a trio of pelicans, the state bird of Louisiana. (For more on Christmas in the Bayou State, turn to page 10.)

Cross-stitch Redbird Ornaments

Materials:
  chart and color key on page 146
  14-count Aida cloth
  embroidery floss (see color key)
  red beads (see color key)
  craft glue
  white bead
  red felt

Work designs on Aida cloth according to chart. Before cutting out design, apply glue to back and along outer edge of worked design to prevent raveling. Let glue dry, and cut out design closely along glue line. Spread another layer of glue on back of cross-stitch design and place on felt. When glue is dry, cut away excess felt.

Embroidered Raccoon Ornament

Materials:
  chart and color key on page 146
  2 (8"-square) pieces cream-colored
    calico fabric
  embroidery floss (see color key)
  Persian yarn (see color key)
  craft knife
  2 (7"-square) pieces mat board
  2 (7"-square) pieces batting
  craft glue
  ½ yard (⅛"-wide) red piping
  8" (⅛"-wide) red satin ribbon

Transfer design to center of one calico square, saving other square for backing. Work all parts of the design with 4 strands of floss and one strand of Persian yarn, except the following: for eyes, nose, and lettering, use 2 strands of floss in colors indicated on chart. Use one strand of floss for all outlining. Block finished embroidery. Add 1" allowance around embroidered oval and cut out. Cut same-size oval for backing.

Cut out 2 ovals each of mat board and batting, according to chart outline. Place embroidered piece face down, place batting over it, and place one mat board oval on top. Apply glue around the top edge of the mat board. Fold fabric over it, clipping curves as necessary, and pressing edges onto glued surface. Let dry.

Glue red piping around the edge of embroidered piece. Make a hanger loop from red satin ribbon and glue to top back of front piece. Assemble back piece in same manner as front piece and glue front and back pieces together.

Needlepoint Pelican Ornaments

Materials (for stocking-shaped ornament):
  chart and color key on page 147
  18-mesh mono canvas (8" x 8½")
  embroidery floss (see color key)
  22" length white cording
  5" x 6½" piece fabric (for backing)
  stuffing

Work design on canvas according to chart. Cut out design, adding a ¼" seam allowance. Knot or tape ends of cording to prevent raveling. Stitch one end of cording to top left of stocking in seam allowance. Transfer stocking pattern to backing fabric and cut out. Turn seam allowances under, leaving an opening at top for stuffing, and slipstitch front to back. Stuff and stitch opening closed. Cross cording at top to make a loop hanger, and stitch cording around edge of ornament to conceal stitches.

Materials (for each round ornament):
  charts and color key on page 147
  18-mesh mono canvas (5½" x 6")
  embroidery floss (see color key)
  15" white cording
  4" x 4½" piece fabric (for backing)
  stuffing

Work design according to chart. Put ornament together same as above.

Christmas Bazaar

Southerners have long been renowned for their fine handwork. In the old days, of course, handwork was a necessity, either because nothing else was available or because people were too poor to buy. Christmas gifts were often handmade and usually practical in nature. (And there have been some hard Christmases in the South, when gifts of any kind were scarce. Stories tell of proud but destitute parents in Civil War days, who—unable to celebrate Christmas as in better times—told their children that the Yankees had captured Santa!)

These days, thank goodness, we do handwork because we love it. And on the following pages, you'll find a wealth of gifts that you can make for your favorite people, very personal presents that will warm hearts in a way that storebought goods never could.

Now's the time to get started. There's a wide selection of gift designs to choose from—toys, home accessories, and personal items—something for almost everyone on your list. And for those closest to you, you can tailor items to individual tastes through the selection of colors and materials.

Don't forget to express appreciation to people who help your day-to-day life go smoothly—your hairdresser, veterinarian, mechanic. Hand out herbed honeys and sherries, or spiced wine and tea. Your own reward will be the feeling of accomplishment you get from creating gifts that show people you care.

Now is the time, too, to start making things in multiples for your favorite bazaar. Whip up these creative contributions— quick-stitched snowflake pillows, doormats festively woven with ribbon, or bags of pungent potpourri—and watch sales soar.

Strawberry Patchwork

Harvest a strawberry patchwork set for the kitchen. Small strips of fabric pieced in rows create a mosaic effect on these pretty accessories, and plump stuffed strawberries on the wreath look ripe for the picking.

ASSEMBLY

For patchwork: all patchwork areas are assembled one horizontal row at a time. Cut all strips 1¼" wide. This includes ¼" seam allowance on each side. Referring to chart, determine the length of each strip by multiplying the number of squares it covers by ¾". Then add ½", regardless of the strip's length, to provide a ¼" seam allowance on each end.

Sew together the strips in one horizontal row, backstitching each piece, and press all seams in same direction. Sew together next horizontal row, and press seams in the opposite direction to avoid bulk. Sew second strip to the first. Continue assembling a row and stitching it to the others, matching edges of designs from one row to the next.

For strawberry seeds: embroider French knots on all strawberries. Use 3 strands of yellow floss, and sew through all layers of fabric, moving from one knot to the next between fabric layers. Use photos as guides on how to scatter knots.

Note: All directions allow for a ¼" seam.

APRON

Materials:
   charts and patterns on page 152
   1¾ yards (45"-wide) bleached muslin
   ¼ yard (45"-wide) green fabric
   ¼ yard (45"-wide) mauve fabric
   white thread
   yellow embroidery floss
   ⅔ yard (¼"-wide) maroon ribbon
   maroon thread

Referring to chart, assemble patchwork for apron bib and skirt. Follow general directions for yellow seeds.

Measure width of apron bib patchwork, and divide measurement in half. If needed, adjust angle of yoke's side edge so that bottom edge matches this measurement. Transfer yoke pattern to muslin, and cut out 2 pieces. (One will be lining.) Cut a piece of muslin the same size as bib patchwork for lining. With right sides facing, place one yoke piece on bib patchwork with straight raw edges even. Stitch together. Open and press. Repeat, to assemble the yoke and patchwork lining.

From bleached muslin, cut 2 waist ties, 3½" x 42", and 2 neck straps, 2" x 22½". Fold waist ties and neck straps in half lengthwise. Stitch along raw edges, leaving one end open to turn. Turn and press.

To keep away from stitching line, roll neck straps to within a few inches of raw edges. Place on front of bib with rolls in center and raw edges even with top of yoke, and pin. Repeat for waist ties, placing them ¼" from bottom edge of patchwork. Place lining face down on straps, ties, and bib, and stitch top and sides. Turn, unroll straps and ties, and press.

Measure width of completed skirt patchwork rectangle, add 2½", and cut a piece of muslin that width x 25". Place skirt patchwork face down on skirt rectangle, with top of patchwork 11½" from one edge and side edges aligned. Stitch along top of patchwork, turn it to front, and press. Turn side and bottom edges of skirt ¼" toward front, and press. Turn again so that these edges form a ½" binding around patchwork, press, and topstitch.

Run 2 rows of gathering stitches ⅛" apart, at top of skirt. Gather to same width as bib, evenly distributing gathers. With right sides facing and raw edges even, sew front piece of bib to skirt. Open, turn raw edge of bib lining under ¼", and blind-stitch to back of skirt.

Tie bow in ribbon and knots in ends, and tack to bib as shown in photo.

PLACE MAT

Materials (makes one mat):
   chart on page 152
   ¼ yard (45"-wide) bleached muslin
   ¾ yard (45"-wide) mauve fabric
   scraps of green fabric
   white thread
   14" x 18" lightweight batting
   1 yard (¼"-wide) maroon ribbon
   maroon thread
   yellow embroidery floss

Referring to chart, assemble patchwork rectangle and borders. Cut batting and piece of mauve fabric same size as top. Layer as for a quilt, and baste together.

From mauve fabric, cut 1¼"-wide bias strips, piecing as necessary, to make a 2-yard-long strip. With right sides facing and raw edges aligned, pin strip around front of mat, smoothing corners. Where ends of strip meet, overlap ½". Turn end that is against mat ¼" to wrong side and press. Stitch strip, and fold to back of mat. Turn edge under ¼", and blind-stitch. Cut ribbon in fourths, tie in bows, and stitch to mat as shown in photo. Follow general directions to embroider seeds.

If you wish, make matching napkins and rings. For napkins, roll-hem 18" squares of muslin. For napkin rings, make a 44" band from green fabric. Make small strawberries as for wreath, tie band in bow around napkins, and attach strawberries as shown in photo.

POT HOLDER

Materials:
   chart on page 152
   ⅛ yard (45"-wide) bleached muslin
   ¼ yard (45"-wide) mauve fabric
   scraps of light green fabric
   white thread
   7½" square of lightweight batting
   1 yard (1/16"-wide) maroon ribbon
   maroon thread
   yellow embroidery floss

Follow chart to assemble patchwork square and borders. Cut a 7½" square of mauve fabric. Layer mauve square, batting, and patchwork as for a quilt. Bring muslin border to back, turn under ¼", then another ¼", and blind-stitch to mauve backing.

For hanger, cut a 1¼" strip of muslin, 4" long. Fold raw edges to center lengthwise. Fold in half lengthwise, and topstitch. Tuck raw edges under, loop, and stitch to a corner of holder. Tie 9" lengths of ribbon in bows, and tack to holder where shown in photo. Follow general directions for yellow seeds.

WREATH

Materials:
  patterns on page 153
  ½ yard (45"-wide) mauve fabric
  white thread
  polyester stuffing
  ⅛ yard (45"-wide) green fabric
  ⅛ yard fusible web fabric
  yellow embroidery floss
  ½ yard (45"-wide) bleached muslin
  Fray Check
  4 yards (¹⁄₁₆"-wide) mauve ribbon
  4 yards (¼"-wide) maroon ribbon
  1 yard (¹⁄₁₆"-wide) maroon ribbon

Transfer patterns for 4 large, one medium, and 7 small strawberries to mauve fabric. Cut out and, with right sides facing, stitch all but tops of berries. Run a gathering stitch close to top opening. Turn, stuff firmly, and pull closed, tucking raw ends inside.

Cut 2 squares of green fabric big enough for 12 caps each, and join, wrong sides facing, with fusible web. Transfer cap pattern to square 12 times, and cut out. Transfer and cut out 8 small and 9 large leaves. With right sides facing, sew together, leaving tops open, and turn. Run a gathering stitch near top openings, pull closed, tucking ends inside, and stitch. Attach caps and leaves to strawberries, following photo. Follow general directions to embroider seeds.

On muslin, draw 2 circles, 15" in diameter, with 4" circles in their centers. Cut out and mark quarters on inside and outside circles with straight pins. Cut a 24" x 4" rectangle from mauve fabric for inner circle and 2 rectangles 45" x 4" for outer circle. Sew short ends of small rectangle together to make small band. Sew 2 rows of gathering stitches, ⅛" apart, along both edges. Mark band in quarters with straight pins.

Sew short ends of 2 large strips together to make a large band. Sew and mark as for small band. Treat raw edges of muslin with Fray Check, and mark quarters. Gather one side of large band to same size as outer edge of muslin circle. Place on muslin, right sides

facing and quarter marks aligned, and stitch together. Repeat process for other side of band. Repeat for one side of inner band. Turn wreath, blind-stitch all but a quarter of remaining seam, and stuff firmly. Blind-stitch closed.

Cut mauve ribbon and ¼"-wide maroon ribbon into 5 lengths, 28" long. Tie around wreath, alternating ribbons and spacing evenly. Tie maroon ribbon's bows on sides of wreath; mauve ribbon's, on back. Cut ¹⁄₁₆"-wide maroon ribbon into 8", 12", and 16" lengths. Tack 3 small berries to ends. Scatter other berries and attach ribbons as shown in photo.

Huggable Knitted Doll

Happily huggable, this knitted doll is a baby any little girl would love. Worked in stockinette stitch, it features bold primary colors accented with festive green.

Materials:
   knitting worsted, 1 skein each in white (A), red (B), and yellow
   no. 9 knitting needles
   2 stitch holders
   small amount of worsted in green (C) and blue
   2 bobbins
   polyester stuffing
   1½ yards (⅛"-wide) green ribbon

Size: 20" high.
Gauge: 4 sts = 1"; 4 rows = 1" in St st.
Note: Entire doll is worked in St st.

FOOT: With A, cast on 6 sts. Rows 1, 3, and 5: Purl. Rows 2 and 4: Inc 1 st, knit across, inc 1 st (end Row 4 with 10 sts). Row 6: Knit. Slip stitches on a holder. Repeat for other foot.

DRESS: With B, cast on 6 sts. From right side, pick up and knit sts of one foot, cast on 4 sts, pick up and work other foot as for first, and cast on 6 sts (36 sts). Work even for 9 rows. Dec 1 st at each end of next k row, then dec 1 st at each end of every 6th row until there are 20 sts left.

Attach C, and work even 3 rows for belt. Slip sts on holder.

ARMS: Wind A onto 2 bobbins to work hands. With one bobbin, cast on 2 sts. Attach B, and cast on 6 sts for sleeves. From right side, pick up dress sts and knit across. Cast on 6 more sts in B and 2 sts from other bobbin (36 sts). Purl back. Inc 1 st each end (color A) of next 3 k rows (42 sts). Dec 1 st each end of next 3 k rows. Next row, bind off remaining sts of hand, and tie off A. Bind off 6 sts of B and work across row. Beg next row, bind off remaining sts of that hand and 6 sts of B. Work across. Bind off 4 sts at beg of next 2 rows (12 sts). Attach C, and work 2 rows for neck.

HEAD: Tie off C, and attach A. Inc 1 st each end of next 5 k rows (22 sts). Work even until piece measures 2½" from neck. Dec each end of next 5 k rows. Bind off 4 sts beg of next 2 rows. Bind off remaining sts.

BACK OF DOLL: Work same as front.

FINISHING: Block both pieces. Using lazy-daisy stitches, follow photo to embroider 1" stars on front and back of doll's skirt. Following photo, use satin stitch outlined with stem stitch to embroider eyes, and stem stitch to embroider mouth. With right sides facing, sew body halves together, leaving an opening for stuffing. Stuff doll firmly, and stitch closed. Use a tapestry needle to weave green ribbon around middle row of waist, under one stitch and over next. Tie in bow in front.

HAIR: Make 2" loops with yellow yarn, and stitch to head for bangs, as shown in photo. Cut 30" lengths of yellow yarn, and center on head from bangs to just above back neckline. Use yellow yarn to stitch in place down center back of head. Gather yarn at each side of head, and braid. Tie tightly with thread, trim ends evenly, and tie green bows over thread. Tack braids to sides of head to hold in place.

Standard Knitting Abbreviations

st(s)—stitch(es)
St st—Stockinette stitch (k 1 row, p 1 row)
inc—increase
k—knit
p—purl
dec—decrease
beg—beginning
"Work even" means to work in pattern stitch without increasing or decreasing.

A Doll with Shaker Simplicity

A simple muslin dress covered by a plain woolen pinafore was the typical daily garb for a Shaker woman. The rope belt around her waist emphasized the Shaker belief in an unadorned, utilitarian existence, which was devoted to work and prayer. The doll-size quilt on the right is a Squares within Squares quilt pattern. All Shaker handiwork had a reputation for fine quality. (For more on Shaker life, see page 24.)

Materials:
   patterns on page 151-153
   1 yard (45″-wide) unbleached muslin
   ⅓ yard (60″-wide) blue wool
   thread to match
   stuffing
   acrylic paint (black and red)
   artist's paintbrush
   1 yard (1″-wide) eyelet lace trim
   1 yard single-fold ecru bias tape
   1 yard of twine or yarn for hair and belt
   8″ x 16″ piece light brown wool

Fold muslin material in half, short ends and right sides together. Transfer doll, dress, sleeve, and pinafore (lining) patterns to wrong side of muslin and cut out. Cut out pinafore and shoe patterns from blue wool.

Stitch front and back of doll body, right sides together, leaving an opening as indicated on pattern. Clip curves, and turn. Stuff legs and arms firmly. Stitch across where arms and legs meet body as indicated on pattern. Finish stuffing body firmly and stitch opening closed. Transfer facial features to doll, paint, and let dry.

To make boots, place 2 boot pieces right sides facing. Leaving top of boot open, stitch around the pieces. Repeat with remaining 2 pieces. Clip curves and turn. Remove threads to fray top edges of boots and stuff. Place doll legs inside boots and hand-stitch tops of boots to legs.

To trim the muslin dress, cut two 6½" pieces each of eyelet lace trim and bias tape. Position raw edges of eyelet trim pieces in fold of bias tape, and stitch. On right side of fabric, stitch bias tape to bottom of dress (front and back). To trim cuffs of sleeves, cut two 3½" pieces each of lace trim and bias tape. For the neck, cut 4½" pieces of each. Stitch lace and bias tape together as before. For sleeves, run a gathering stitch at cuff edges and gather to 3½". Stitch bias tape and lace trim (ruffle down) to right sides of gathered cuffs. For neck, stitch the 4½" pieces of bias tape and lace trim to the right side of neck edges (ruffle up). Stitch front and back of dress, right sides together, at shoulder seams. Gather tops of sleeves to fit armholes. Pin sleeves to armholes, right sides together, and stitch. With right sides together, start at dress bottom and stitch side seams, continuing down sleeves. Turn and iron. Stitch 2 white buttons at the neck. Slip dress over doll head, and blind-stitch neck ruffle seams.

For pinafore, fold all edges of muslin and wool pieces ¼" to wrong side, mitering corners, and iron. Place one piece of muslin and one piece of wool wrong sides together. Leaving shoulder edges open, topstitch around entire piece. Repeat with remaining pieces of muslin and wool. Slip back straps

slightly inside front straps and blind-stitch shoulders together. Slip pinafore over doll head, wind a 25" length of twine several times around waist and tie.

To make scarf and hair, cut a 5½" x 6½" piece of blue wool and two 4" lengths of twine. Turn one long side of scarf piece ¼" to wrong side and iron. With wrong side up, place twine on pressed edge as shown in Diagram 1, and stitch so that thread catches parts of the twine. Fray the 3 raw edges of scarf. Place scarf on doll head with center of finished edge at center front. Bring scarf ends around head to the nape of the neck and tack.

For quilted square, transfer triangle pattern and cut out 4 brown pieces and 4 blue pieces from wool. Using a ⅛" seam, stitch triangles together to form four 2-color squares. From brown wool, cut two 1¾" x 3¼" strips and two 1¾" x 5¼" strips. From blue wool, cut two 1¾" x 5½" strips and two 1¾" x 7½" strips. As shown in Diagram 2, piece center block and strips together with a ¼" seam. Iron. Place pieced work on 7½" x 8" piece of brown wool. Topstitch ¼" outside of brown border and ¼" from all seams within square. Even edges and fray.

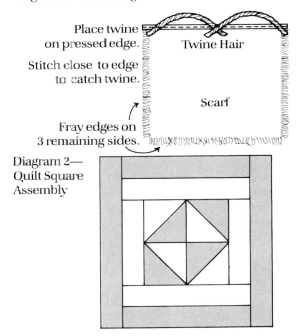

Diagram 1—Attaching Twine Hair to Scarf

Place twine on pressed edge.

Twine Hair

Stitch close to edge to catch twine.

Scarf

Fray edges on 3 remaining sides.

Diagram 2— Quilt Square Assembly

Magnolias Blossom Year-Round

One of the harbingers of spring in the South is the arrival of the cream-colored, magnificently fragrant magnolia blossom. Discover the year-round, never-wilt variety of this gracious Southern icon in soft sculpture.

Leaves and petals are fashioned from fabric. Topstitching and contour quilting add depth and realism to the design. Cover a wreath form or adorn a wooden box with the bloom to remind yourself that, whether you live in Mississippi or Minnesota, your heart can be in Dixie.

MAGNOLIA WREATH

Materials:
   patterns on page 150
   60"-wide pinwale corduroy: 1 yard
      cream, 1 yard tan, 1 yard maroon,
      1½ yards green
   thread to match
   20" wire wreath form
   craft glue or hot glue gun
   1½ yards batting
   10 yards (#18) florist's wire
   1 yard gold gimp
   long needle

Cut a 5"-wide strip across the width of green corduroy fabric. Lay it right side down in a circle, and place wreath form on top. Bring fabric up and around wreath form, and glue fabric to metal, covering the frame, except for a 1½" square area left of center where blossom will fit into frame.

To make large leaves, transfer large leaf pattern to corduroy, and cut 7 leaves from green, 4 from tan, and 3 from maroon. For small leaves, transfer small leaf pattern to corduroy, and cut 8 leaves from green, 4 from tan, and 4 from maroon. Cut 8 small leaves from batting. (Large leaves need no batting.) Place a large green leaf on a large maroon or tan leaf, right sides facing. Leaving the bottom open, stitch together with a ¼" seam. Clip corners and turn. Repeat with all large leaves. Place a small green leaf on a small maroon or tan leaf, right sides facing, with batting on bottom. Stitch same as above. Clip curves, and turn. Repeat with all small leaves.

Transfer vein markings onto green side of leaves (or stitch freehand). With green thread, topstitch along lines. (Center vein should allow for wire insertion.) Insert an 8" length of wire into center of all large and 6 small leaves, allowing wire to extend 1" below base. Turn wires and raw edges of fabric to inside of leaf. Gather fabric and stitch closed. Insert a 20" length of wire into the 2 remaining small leaves, allowing 12" of wire to extend below base. Fold raw edges of fabric to inside, and hand-stitch around wire extensions.

For magnolia petals, fold cream corduroy in half, right sides facing and short ends together. Transfer large petal pattern to fabric and cut out 9 pairs of petals. Cut 9 petals from batting. With right sides of corduroy pairs facing and batting on bottom, stitch according to above directions for small leaves. Clip curves and turn. Cut nine 21" lengths of wire. Insert wire at bottom and shape along petal seams, pinning in place as you go. Using cream thread and beginning ½" in from wire, topstitch around edge of petal, forming a casing for wire. Continue stitching evenly spaced rows of contour quilting toward center of each petal, as in photograph. Twist wire ends together and tuck inside petal.

To make stamen, cut 2 triangles (4" sides and 5" base), from cream corduroy. With right sides facing, stitch triangles (leaving base open), turn, and stuff. Gather base, forming a cone shape, and stitch closed. Starting at top, wind gimp around cone, overlapping edges and stitching until cone is covered. Around base, form several loops with braid, and stitch in place.

Starting with 3 magnolia petals as the center, gather petals 2″ above their bases, and stitch back and forth to secure petals to each other. Continue adding remaining petals in same way, spacing evenly around center to make blossom. Pin stamen to center of blossom, and stitch in place.

Twist a 10″ length of wire tightly around base of magnolia blossom, and secure it to wreath form at opening in corduroy cover. To make blossom more stable, push base of blossom into spaces between wires on wreath. Attach the long-wired leaves to blossom base, allowing them to extend past the blossom. See Diagram. Position leaves around wreath form as shown in Diagram.

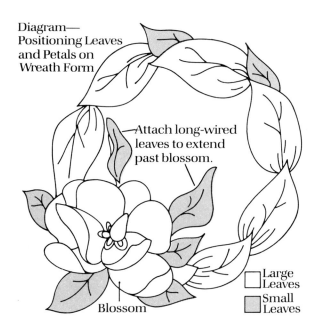

Diagram—
Positioning Leaves
and Petals on
Wreath Form

Attach long-wired leaves to extend past blossom.

Blossom

☐ Large Leaves
◩ Small Leaves

Using craft glue or glue gun, attach leaves to each other and wire form, overlapping to conceal form and leaf ends. Bend wired shapes into a natural position. Cut a 10′ length of wire, and make a loop hanger at top of wreath form.

MAGNOLIA BOX

Materials:
   patterns on page 150
   oval wooden box with lid
   60″-wide pinwale corduroy: ⅓ yard cream, ½ yard green, scraps of tan and maroon
   thread to match
   hot glue gun
   3⅓ yards (½″-wide) decorative green braid
   ½ yard batting
   14 feet (#18) florist's wire
   long needle
   1 yard gold gimp

Cover box with green corduroy to point where it meets rim of lid. Cover lid. Glue decorative braid over raw edges of fabric on lid and box.

To make magnolia blossom, use small petal pattern. Fold cream fabric in half, short sides together, and right sides facing. Transfer pattern to corduroy, and cut out 9 pairs of petals. To make leaves, use small leaf pattern, and cut out 3 green leaves. Using same pattern, cut 2 from maroon fabric and one from tan fabric. Assemble, stitch, and wire petals and leaves in same manner as for wreath. Stitch petals together ¼″ above their bases. Arrange blossom. Following above instructions, make stamen and attach to center of blossom.

Arrange magnolia blossom and leaves on top of box, allowing leaves to drape slightly over sides. Attach to covered lid with glue gun. Bend wires in leaves and blossoms for a natural look.

Gussied-Up Geese

Not all geese fly south for the winter. And though you can't serve them for Christmas dinner, this wooden trio deserves to be on show for the holidays and all year. These plucky ladies are ready to promenade across your table, mantel, or window sill, without making so much as a squawk.

Even a beginning painter can wield a brush freehand to achieve the rustic folk-art details that add so much character. The simple wooden cutouts become gussied-up geese when you decorate them in such finery as we show here. Beribboned hats to match their bright aprons lead us to believe these geese are on their way somewhere— perhaps to a party of their own.

Reduce the pattern, and make baby geese to trail behind, or increase the amount of wood you use, to make an entire gaggle of geese.

Materials (for three geese):
 pattern on page 154
 21″ of 1″ x 12″ white pine
 band saw or jigsaw
 sandpaper
 wood sealer
 acrylic paints (white, red, black, gold, maroon)
 wood glue
 water-based varnish

Transfer patterns to wood and cut out. Sand and apply a coat of sealer. Let dry. Paint all sides of cutouts white. Transfer painting details to cutouts (or paint freehand if desired). Paint front and back, following photograph. Let dry. Attach stands to bottom of geese with wood glue and let dry. Paint stands. Apply a coat of varnish and allow to dry thoroughly.

Laced with Ribbon: A Holiday Doormat

By simply lacing with ribbon, you can prettify a practical, everyday doormat, turning it into a festive entryway decoration. It's so easy and inexpensive to do, you'll want to make one for yourself and all your neighborhood friends. These mats are ideal for hostess gifts for your out-of-town holiday visits, and for bazaar offerings as well.

You can buy these mats at most large discount stores and many hardware stores. Look for rice straw mats with a braided edge (see photo). You'll need weatherproof ribbon, available at florist's shops or specialty display shops. To estimate the amount of ribbon needed to weave around your mat, measure all 4 sides. Add the measurements plus 15". Buy this amount of ⅞"-wide ribbon. For the bow, you'll need 2 yards of 2⅝"-wide ribbon.

Begin weaving by pulling the ribbon from the back of the mat through a hole anywhere along edge. Leave 3" excess ribbon on the back, to tie to other ribbon end after weaving. (All weaving will be done on the top edge of the mat.) Following the parallel slanted straws on the outside top edge of the mat's braid, weave under 1, over 2. (Weave loosely so that ribbon will show up.) Continue this pattern, except to go under the slanted straws directly on the corners, even if you have to skip straws to do it. When you have encircled the mat with ribbon, pull remaining ribbon to the back of the mat and tie ends together.

To make a bow from the wider ribbon, wrap it around an 8" square of cardboard. Holding ribbon in the center, slide it off the cardboard. At the center of the ribbon, cut Vs from each side, being careful not to cut all the way through. Twist a pipe cleaner or chenille stem around Vs to secure bow at center. At a corner, stick ends of pipe cleaner through mat to the back. Twist ends together to secure bow.

Quick-Stitch a Snowflake

Rug yarn and a large needle make oversized colonial knots, so you can quickly plot the crystals of this snowflake. A graphic seasonal emblem (six-sided as snowflakes generally are), it stands out brightly on a red pillow. (Other deep colors would also make good backgrounds.) When one of these fluffy snowflake pillows lights on a sofa or chair, it sends out warm and welcoming signals to guests. And for your contribution to a bazaar, it's a cinch to stitch up a blizzard of these easy-to-make pillows.

To make a snowflake pillow, fold an 18" x 36" piece of fabric in half, short sides together. Cut in two equal pieces. With a water-soluble fabric pen, draw a 14" square (the pillow top) in the center of one fabric square. Trace pattern on page 149 and center on pillow top.

Place fabric in an embroidery hoop or frame. To stitch design, you'll need a skein of white rug yarn. With one strand of yarn in a large tapestry or darning needle, work design from center of snowflake out, with a colonial knot stitch (see Diagram on page 137). When completed, remove snowflake pattern lines with water and press.

To finish pillow, you'll need 2 yards white fabric-covered cording. Leaving a little excess cording at the beginning, baste cording around pillow top, with cording facing in and raw edges aligned. Overlap cording at end. With right sides facing, pin remaining fabric square to pillow top. Stitch together along basting line, leaving an opening to turn. Trim seam and clip corners. Turn and press. Fill firmly with stuffing and slipstitch opening closed.

Right: The snowflake design on this pillow is created with the colonial knot stitch, a mainstay of the revived art of candlewicking.

Woodcutter's Workmates

Practical and sturdy doesn't have to mean plain. Take this work apron and log carrier: rays of chamois crisscross the denim flap of the apron and one side of the log carrier. Bright orange topstitching spices up the blue-jean style of the pieces.

And the apron's pockets are so simple to stitch, it will be easy to adapt them to suit the needs of that active man on your list. Maybe your thoughtfulness will be repaid when it's time to take the tree down and chop it up for kindling!

APRON

Materials:
  ⅔ yard (48"-wide) blue denim
  orange, chamois-colored thread
  small piece of chamois
  fabric glue

Note: All topstitching will be in 2 parallel rows, ¼" apart.

Wash and iron denim. From denim, cut 10" x 20" apron flap, 9" x 20" flap pocket, 11" square bib, 8" square bib pocket, 2 waist ties 2" x 30", and one neck strap 2" wide and long enough to fit recipient. (Bib piece can also be enlarged, if needed, for a better fit.)

With orange thread, zigzag-stitch edge of one long side of flap pocket. Fold edge under ⅝", press, and topstitch 2 rows close to fold. This side is top of pocket.

Following Diagram, mark appliqué lines on pocket and cut strips of chamois 1¼" wide and length of lines. Glue chamois strips in place, and trim edges even with edges of pocket. Use matching thread to zigzag-stitch strips to pocket.

Lay pocket on flap, matching remaining long raw edge of pocket with one raw edge of flap. Zigzag-stitch all raw edges of flap, stitching pocket in place. Turn bottom edge under ⅝", press, and topstitch as above. Turn flap and pocket sides under ⅝" and topstitch. Turn remaining side of flap under ⅝" and topstitch. Mark pocket in thirds vertically (see Diagram) and topstitch.

Zigzag-stitch one edge of bib pocket. Fold under ½", press, and topstitch. Fold remaining pocket edges under ½" and press. Pin pocket to center of bib with topstitched edge at top. Topstitch sides and bottom of pocket to bib. Topstitch 2 pencil pockets 1" wide on bib pocket (see Diagram). Zigzag edges of bib, fold under ⅝", press, and topstitch.

Zigzag-stitch one long edge of straps. Fold in thirds (about ¾" wide) with zigzagged edge overlapping raw edge, and topstitch down center. Zigzag-tack waist ties to top corners of flap and neck strap to top corners of bib.

Pin bib to center top of flap, overlapping bib on front of flap. Stitch together along bib's topstitched lines.

LOG CARRIER

Materials:
**1 yard (48"-wide) blue denim
orange, chamois-colored thread
piece of chamois (at least 24" long)
fabric glue**

Note: All topstitching will be in 2 parallel rows, ¼" apart.

Wash and iron denim. From denim, cut 24" x 41" rectangle for carrier and 2 strips 3" x 48" for handles. Fold long sides of rectangle under ⅝" and press. Fold under again, and topstitch with orange thread. Fold short sides under 1⅝" and press. Fold under 1⅝" again and press. Topstitch about 1¼" from edge of carrier.

For chamois appliqué, mark random diagonal lines on one half of carrier. Cut strips of chamois 1¼" wide and length of lines. Glue strips to carrier, and trim edges even with edges of carrier. Use matching thread to zigzag-stitch strips to carrier.

Zigzag-stitch one long edge of handles. Fold in thirds, zigzagged edge overlapping raw edges, and topstitch along both long sides. On outside of carrier, draw a line parallel to and 7" from one long side. Repeat for other side. Loop and pin handles along these lines (loop will extend beyond carrier) so that all raw edges meet in middle (bottom of carrier). To secure handles, sew reinforcing squares of stitching 7" from short sides of carrier. Stitch an X through each square. Topstitch handles to carrier between X squares, following previous stitching lines.

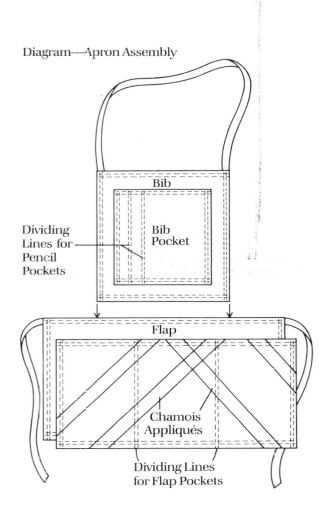

Diagram—Apron Assembly

Bib

Dividing Lines for Pencil Pockets

Bib Pocket

Flap

Chamois Appliqués

Dividing Lines for Flap Pockets

Spice is Nice

Many Christmas memories are tied to poignant encounters with flavor and aroma, riots of the senses incited by spicy-sweet teasers of the season. A collection of tantalizing recipes—nose-quivering, mouthwatering concoctions—to prepare for friends and neighbors, or to offer as bazaar items, is assembled here. And in the process of brewing and blending these aromatic giveaways, there's a fortunate fringe benefit for you: your own house will be permeated with the scents that spice the holidays.

CHRISTMAS POTPOURRI

Materials: (Exact ingredient amounts are not given, because they may vary depending on materials available. Results will be pleasing in any combination of the following.)
> small pinecones and needles
> sweet-gum balls
> dried acorns and chestnuts
> broken cinnamon sticks
> whole cloves, star anise, ginger root
> cracked nutmegs
> coriander seeds
> beechnut husks
> bay, eucalyptus, and patchouli leaves
> sandalwood pieces
> dried rose hips and red strawflower petals
> patchouli, pine or spruce, and sandalwood oils
> glass container with a lid

Mix dried ingredients together for desired amount of potpourri. For every 4 cups of dried mixture, add 2 drops of each of the oils. Mix well, cover, and allow 4-6 weeks for the scents to marry. To preserve scent, place in a glass container with a lid, and uncover when you want to freshen the air. To release scent, gently squeeze the mixture.

Above: This refreshing potpourri is designed for the season, not light and flowery, but hearty with herbs, spices, and essential oils. Woodsy staples—nuts, pinecones and needles, and sweet-gum balls—contribute texture.

78

Above: For an unusual and practical trivet, wire cinnamon sticks together in a star shape. When a hot pot is placed on the star, the fragrance of cinnamon is released. Or arrange smaller stars on a wreath form, or string them together in a garland, and enjoy the heady scent of cinnamon throughout the holidays.

CINNAMON-STICK TRIVETS

Materials:
- **4 feet copper or noncorrosive wire**
- **10 (3″-long) cinnamon sticks**
- **5 (1½″-long) cinnamon sticks**

Cut a 33″ length of wire and thread all ten 3″ cinnamon sticks onto wire. Twist ends of wire together to form a loop. Cut an 11″ length of wire and thread the 1½″ cinnamon sticks onto it. Attach one end of the short wire between cinnamon sticks and continue attaching short wire as shown in Diagram, until a complete star is formed. Make trivets to fit any size pan or casserole dish by altering the lengths of wire and cinnamon sticks.

Diagram—Assembly of Cinnamon-Stick Star Trivet

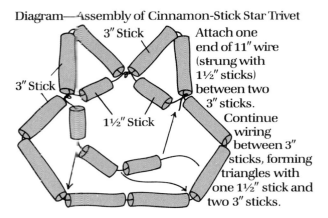

3″ Stick

3″ Stick

1½″ Stick

Attach one end of 11″ wire (strung with 1½″ sticks) between two 3″ sticks. Continue wiring between 3″ sticks, forming triangles with one 1½″ stick and two 3″ sticks.

Above: For pungent condiments, pour hot honey over sprigs of fresh herbs to make a taste sensation. Or allow sherry to age with a sprig in the bottle. Use herbal sherry in soup, stew, or casserole recipes that call for sherry, or stir it into hot bouillon for a savory drink. Identify contents of jars and bottles with decorative labels.

HERBAL SHERRY

Materials:
   **fresh sprigs of desired herbs
      (recommended herbs—basil, sage,
      rosemary, lovage, and tarragon)**
   **narrow-necked bottles with corks or
      caps**
   drinking straw
   **dry sherry (light or aged, to your
      taste)**
   decorative paper label

Note: The ideal time for harvesting home-grown herbs is on a clear sunny morning, right after the dew has dried on the leaves. And if the plant is just opening its flowers, that's even better.

Place a fresh herb sprig in the bottle, using the drinking straw to push it through the narrow neck of the bottle. Pour in the sherry, close the bottle, and allow to age 2-3 weeks. Taste. If the flavor is not intense enough, remove the herb sprig and replace it with a fresh one, and repeat aging time. For visual appeal, leave the herb sprig in the bottle. Label sherry bottle, identifying the herb flavor.

HERBAL HONEY

Materials:
   mild-flavored honey
   **fresh sprigs of desired herbs
      (recommended herbs—lemon
      verbena, lemon thyme, sage, mint,
      rosemary, thyme, lavender leaves
      and flowers, scented geranium
      leaves, especially rose)**
   glass jar with cap
   decorative paper label

See note on harvesting homegrown herbs under Herbal Sherry.

Pour 1 cup honey into a pot and heat until liquified. Place a fresh herb sprig in the jar. Pour in the hot liquified honey and place the cap on the jar. Allow to age for a week or more. Taste. If the flavor is not intense enough, remove the herb sprig and replace it with a fresh one, and repeat the aging time. The hot honey will wilt the leaves, so before giving as a gift, replace the herb sprig with a fresh one. Label the honey jar, identifying the herb flavor. Three honey jars, each with a different herb flavor, make a nice gift set.

SPICED-TEA GIFT PACKAGE

Combine first 6 ingredients listed in recipe below. (Use a nutcracker to crush spices as necessary.) Place in a muslin drawstring bag. Attach bag and recipe card to tin of loose black tea.

Spiced Tea:
- **4 tablespoons crushed cardamom pods**
- **½ teaspoon whole cloves**
- **1 broken stick cinnamon**
- **6 peppercorns**
- **1 crushed small fresh nutmeg**
- **2 teaspoons ground ginger**
  - **black tea**
- **4 cups milk**
- **8 tablespoons honey, or to taste**

Brew tea by pouring 4 cups boiling water over 4 teaspoons tea in pot. Strain, return to pot, and add milk, honey, and spice bag. Bring to a very slow simmer over low heat, cook 10 minutes, remove spice bag. Garnish with fresh ginger, if desired. Serves 8 cups.

SPICED-CIDER GIFT PACKAGE

Place 1½ tablespoons whole cloves in a muslin drawstring bag and pull string tight. Tie bag string around 3 cinnamon sticks. Attach bag and recipe card to apple cider, as for Mulled Wine.

Hot Spiced Cider:
- **1 gallon apple cider**
- **1½ tablespoons whole cloves**
- **3 cinnamon sticks**
- **1 lemon, cut in 6 slices**

Remove 6 cloves from bag and place one in the center of each lemon slice. Close bag. Pour cider into a large pot, add spice bag and cinnamon sticks, and float lemon slices. Simmer for 15 minutes. Remove lemon slices and place in mugs. Remove bag and cinnamon, fill mugs, and serve.

Above: To spice up beverages, make fragrant blends, place in muslin bags with drawstrings, and tie to bottles of wine or cider, or tins of tea. Attach a recipe card to each.

MULLED-WINE GIFT PACKAGE

Combine first 5 ingredients listed in recipe below. (Use a nutcracker to crush spices as necessary.) Place spice mixture in a muslin bag with a drawstring. Tie bag around the neck of a bottle of burgundy wine. (If desired, first wrap bottle in a purchased paper wine sack or stitch one from fabric.) Write recipe on a recipe card. Punch a hole in the card, insert ribbon through hole, and tie card to neck of bottle.

Mulled Wine:
- **1 broken cinnamon stick**
- **4 crushed cardamom pods**
- **1 crushed fresh nutmeg**
- **1 strip dried orange peel**
- **6 whole cloves**
- **1 quart burgundy wine**
- **1 orange, sliced**

Place wine and bag containing above spices in pot. Add end slices of orange. Simmer 10-15 minutes. Remove spice bag and orange slices. Place remaining orange slices in heat-resistant glasses or mugs, fill with hot wine, and serve.

Add Punch to a Simple Box

A simple wooden box, handy for storing everything from sewing items to spare pocket change, becomes a handcrafted treasure when topped with copper foil punched in a pattern of dots. At first glance, the motif appears to be a flowery abstract of curving lines, but close study reveals two doves captured in midflight. Best of all, the intricate finished design belies the ease of copper punching.

Transfer the pattern on page 142 to tracing paper with a black pen. Tape a 10″

square of tooling foil to newspaper and then tape pattern on top of it. (Pattern is designed to fit a round, wooden box with a lid 9½″ in diameter.)

With a copper-punching tool or an ice-pick, punch holes through pattern into foil. Remove completed punched foil from newspaper and, with tacks, position on box lid. Trim foil to fit and remove tacks. Apply cement glue ⅛″ from edge of lid top and secure foil to lid. Glue ribbon or lace (you'll need about a yard) to cover raw edge of foil.

Celebrations from the Kitchen

For children and adults alike, Christmas would not be the same without a tantalizing array of favorite foods. To walk into a house and be met with the unmistakable aroma of your favorite pecan pie or sweet potato casserole (with marshmallows on top) is to be flooded with memories of past holidays and welcomed home even faster than with the kisses and bear hugs that are next to come.

Lured by the irresistible scents of bread baking or cakes cooling, guests and family can often be found gathered in the kitchen, talking and tasting. An extra hand to pack cookies in a tin (three for them, one for me) or the stray finger allowed to graze the inside of the icing bowl—these are useful barometers of gastronomic success. And experienced cooks acknowledge such pilferage as a tribute to their fare.

Sampling remains the key to cooking, so taste everything within reach. By trying new as well as old reliable recipes, you can enliven your holiday menu and broaden your guests' palates.

That's just where this chapter can help you. Explore the menus and individual recipes here for mouth-watering appetizers, specially selected meats and vegetable accompaniments, and desserts worthy of applause. Try the sweet English trifle, cook up a Cajun feast, or any of a dozen possibilities. We also offer an abundance of beverage and gift ideas to relieve you of the frantic search for that perfect recipe to fit your expression of the holiday and your schedule. And our medley of cakes, pies, bread, and candies, ranging from epicurean delights to quick snacks, will entice guests of all ages.

However you choose to celebrate—from a large soirée for those who have come from afar to an intimate gathering of your family—the assortment of menus and viands in this chapter are certain to suit the style and expectations of this most festive time.

A Warm Welcome

With a buffet-style menu like the one here (a festive board of appetizers and a coffee/dessert bar), you can share your holiday hospitality with many more friends than you could with a sit-down dinner. And imagine your home filled with the smiling faces and happy chatter of your favorite folks, mixing, mingling, and munching your fancy fare. That satisfying scene could be one of your most fulfilling experiences of the season.

Old-Fashioned Wassail
Coffee Bar
Crab-Stuffed Cherry Tomatoes
Flank Steak Rolls with
Horseradish Sauce
Chutney Cheese Pâté   Crackers
Cucumber Canapés
Apricot Puffs
Holiday Rosettes
English Trifle
(Menu serves 20-24.)

Coffee becomes an adventure when partnered with savory condiments and luscious liqueurs. Place desserts, such as the Holiday Rosettes shown here, nearby.

OLD-FASHIONED WASSAIL

 1 tablespoon whole cloves
 1 (3-inch) stick cinnamon
 2 quarts apple cider or apple juice
 1 quart cranapple juice
 1 (46-ounce) can pineapple juice
 1 (12-ounce) can frozen orange juice concentrate, thawed and undiluted
 1 (6-ounce) can frozen lemonade concentrate, thawed and undiluted
 1 cup plus 2 tablespoons water
 ⅔ cup firmly packed brown sugar
 ½ cup sugar

Tie cloves and cinnamon in a cheesecloth bag. Place spice bag and remaining ingredients in a large kettle; stir well. Bring to a boil; reduce heat and simmer, uncovered, 15 minutes. Remove the spice bag. Yield: 1½ gallons.

COFFEE BAR

Instead of serving plain coffee, set up a coffee bar near the dessert table. Brew the coffee with slivered almonds or strips of orange peel for added flavor. Set out brandy or several of your favorite liqueurs to stir into the coffee, such as kirsch, Galliano, Kahlúa, Triple Sec, Tia Maria, or amaretto. Offer sugar cubes, whipped cream, and grated chocolate, and serve with cinnamon stick stirrers. Add strawberries or maraschino cherries to garnish a cloud of whipped cream on top.

CRAB-STUFFED CHERRY TOMATOES

 ½ cup cooked crabmeat
 2 tablespoons lemon juice
 1 teaspoon Worcestershire sauce
 1 tablespoon finely chopped green onions
 ½ teaspoon dried whole tarragon
 1 small clove garlic, minced
 ⅛ teaspoon red pepper
 ⅛ teaspoon freshly ground pepper
24 cherry tomatoes
    Salt
 1 (3-ounce) package cream cheese, softened
 1 tablespoon milk
 1 tablespoon chopped fresh parsley
    Fresh parsley sprigs

Drain crabmeat well by pressing between paper towels; flake crabmeat with a fork. Combine crabmeat and next 7 ingredients; stir well. Cover and chill.

Wash tomatoes thoroughly. Cut a thin slice from top of each tomato; carefully scoop out pulp, reserving pulp for other uses. Sprinkle shells lightly with salt, and invert onto a paper towel-lined baking sheet. Chill until needed.

Drain crab mixture well. Beat cream cheese and milk until fluffy; stir in crab mixture and chopped parsley. Spoon mixture into tomato shells. Garnish with parsley. Yield: 2 dozen.

FLANK STEAK ROLLS WITH HORSERADISH SAUCE

 ½ cup vegetable oil
 ¼ cup vinegar
 1 tablespoon Worcestershire sauce
 1 (1.25-ounce) envelope onion soup mix
 ½ teaspoon sugar
 3 pounds flank steak
    Horseradish Sauce
    Commercial party rolls

Your guests can make a meal from this array of appetizers. From front, Chutney Cheese Pâté, Cucumber Canapés, Crab-Stuffed Cherry Tomatoes, and Flank Steak Rolls with Horseradish Sauce.

Combine first 5 ingredients in a shallow dish, mixing well. Add steak, turning to coat both sides. Cover and marinate at least 8 hours or overnight in refrigerator, turning one time.

Remove steak from marinade. Grill over hot coals about 10 minutes on each side or to desired degree of doneness; baste frequently with marinade. Slice steak across grain into thin slices. Serve with Horseradish Sauce and party rolls. Yield: about 2½ dozen appetizer sandwiches.

Horseradish Sauce:

- 2 **teaspoons prepared horseradish**
- ½ **teaspoon minced fresh dillweed**
- ¼ **teaspoon garlic salt**
- ¾ **cup whipping cream, whipped**
  Sprig of fresh dill (optional)

Fold horseradish, ½ teaspoon dillweed, and garlic salt into whipped cream. Spoon into a serving dish; garnish with dill, if desired. Yield: about 1½ cups.

CHUTNEY CHEESE PÂTÉ

- 2 **(8-ounce) packages cream cheese, softened**
- 1½ **cups (6 ounces) shredded sharp Cheddar cheese**
- 1 **cup (4 ounces) shredded Swiss cheese**
- 3½ **tablespoons dry sherry**
- 1¼ **teaspoons curry powder**
- 1 **cup chutney**
- 1 **to 2 green onions with tops, finely chopped**
  Red pepper strips

Combine softened cream cheese, sharp Cheddar cheese, Swiss cheese, dry sherry, and curry powder; beat at medium speed of an electric mixer until blended. Shape mixture into a 10-inch circle on a 12-inch round serving dish; cover and chill until firm. Spread chutney over cheese mixture; sprinkle with green onion, and garnish with red pepper strips. Serve with assorted crackers. Yield: about 5 cups.

CUCUMBER CANAPÉS

1 large cucumber
1 (3-ounce) package cream cheese, softened
3 tablespoons butter, softened
2 tablespoons crumbled blue cheese, softened
½ cup finely chopped cooked ham
¼ cup finely chopped red pepper
¼ cup finely chopped green onions
3 tablespoons chopped walnuts
2 tablespoons finely chopped sweet pickle
Red pepper strips

Score cucumber with the tines of a fork. Slice into ¼-inch slices. Set aside.

Combine cream cheese, butter, and blue cheese, beating well. Add remaining ingredients except red pepper strips, stirring until blended. Spread on cucumber slices. Garnish with red pepper strips. Yield: 2 to 2½ dozen.

Note: Cream cheese mixture may also be spread on party rye or wheat bread.

APRICOT PUFFS

½ cup cream-style cottage cheese
½ cup butter or margarine, softened
1 cup all-purpose flour
1 (6-ounce) package dried apricots
½ cup sugar
½ cup water
¾ cup ground pecans or almonds
2 tablespoons sugar
1 egg white, lightly beaten

Combine cottage cheese, butter, and flour; stir until blended. Refrigerate at least 8 hours.

Combine apricots, ½ cup sugar, and water in a heavy saucepan; cook over low heat, stirring occasionally, about 20 minutes or until apricots are tender. Cool. Position knife blade in food processor bowl; add apricots. Top with cover; process about 30 seconds or until minced.

Roll pastry to ⅛-inch thickness on a lightly floured surface. Cut into 2-inch circles. Spoon ½ teaspoon apricot mixture on half of each pastry circle; fold in half, making sure edges are even. Press pastry edges firmly together using a fork dipped in flour.

Combine pecans and 2 tablespoons sugar. Brush dough with egg white, and roll in pecan mixture. Place on lightly greased cookie sheets. Bake at 375° for 12 to 15 minutes or until lightly browned. Yield: 4 dozen.

HOLIDAY ROSETTES

1 cup plus 1 tablespoon all-purpose flour
1 cup milk
1 egg
1 tablespoon sugar
1 tablespoon vanilla extract
½ teaspoon salt
Vegetable oil
Sifted powdered sugar

Combine first 6 ingredients; beat at low speed of an electric mixer until blended and smooth. Cover and chill mixture 30 minutes or overnight.

Heat about 2 inches oil to 370° in a medium saucepan. Heat rosette iron in hot oil 1 minute. Drain excess oil from iron; dip into batter (do not coat top of iron with batter).

Dip iron into hot oil. As soon as rosette is formed (5 to 10 seconds), lift iron slowly up and down to release rosette from iron. Cook until golden, turning once. Remove from oil, and drain on paper towels.

Reheat iron in oil for a few seconds, and repeat procedure for each rosette, stirring batter occasionally. Sprinkle rosettes with powdered sugar. Yield: 3½ dozen.

ENGLISH TRIFLE

  1 **cup butter or margarine, softened**
  ½ **cup shortening**
  3 **cups sugar**
  5 **eggs**
  3 **cups all-purpose flour**
  1 **teaspoon baking powder**
  1 **cup milk**
  1 **teaspoon vanilla extract**
  1 **teaspoon lemon extract**
  ¾ **cup cream sherry, divided**
1½ **cups fresh strawberries, hulled**
    and halved
    Boiled custard (recipe follows)
  1 **cup strawberry preserves**
1½ **cups whipping cream, whipped**
  ¼ **cup plus 2 tablespoons sifted**
    powdered sugar
    Fresh whole strawberries

Cream butter and shortening; gradually add sugar, beating well at medium speed of an electric mixer. Add eggs, one at a time, beating after each addition.

Combine flour and baking powder; add to creamed mixture alternately with milk, beginning and ending with flour mixture; mix well after each addition. Stir in flavorings.

Pour batter into a greased and floured 10-inch tube pan. Bake at 350° for 1 hour and 15 minutes or until a wooden pick inserted in center comes out clean. Cool in pan 10 to 15 minutes; remove from pan, and cool completely on a wire rack.

Slice cake into ¼-inch slices; trim and discard crust. Line the bottom of a 16-cup trifle bowl with one-third of cake slices; sprinkle with ¼ cup sherry. Arrange strawberry halves, cut side out, around lower edge of bowl. Spoon 2 cups boiled custard over cake slices; place half of remaining cake slices over custard. Gently spread strawberry preserves over cake; top with remaining cake slices. Pour remaining sherry over trifle. Spoon remaining custard on top. Cover and chill 3 to 4 hours.

Beat whipping cream until foamy; gradually add powdered sugar, beating until soft peaks form. Spread over trifle; garnish with whole strawberries. Serve immediately. Yield: 16 to 18 servings.

Boiled Custard:

  2 **cups milk**
  ⅔ **cup whipping cream**
  4 **eggs**
  ⅔ **cup sugar**
  ½ **teaspoon vanilla extract**

Combine milk and whipping cream in a medium saucepan; cook over low heat until warm. Combine eggs and sugar, beating well. Gradually stir about one-fourth of warm mixture into eggs; add to remaining hot mixture, stirring constantly.

Cook over low heat, stirring constantly, until mixture thickens and coats the spoon. Remove from heat; stir in vanilla. Cool to room temperature; chill. Yield: 3½ cups.

Christmas Dinner with Cajun Spice

Conjure the Cajun love of food and occasion when you lay delicious south Louisiana fare before your loved ones this year. John Folse, owner-chef of Lafitte's Landing in Donaldsonville, Louisiana, offers these savory recipes for a memorable Christmas dinner.

Louisiana Seafood Gumbo
Baked Goose
Pecan-Rice Dressing
Shrimp-Stuffed Mirlitons
Brandied Sweet Potatoes
Floating Island Custard
Cajun Pralines
Café au Lait
(Menu serves 8.)

Above: Lafitte's Landing owner-chef, John Folse, second from right, shares food and holiday cheer with co-worker Cindy Esquivel, assistant chef Leon Lemoine, and good friend Gaston Hirsch. A bona fide Cajun, Folse blends classical French cuisine and traditional Cajun and Creole cooking. In competition, his gumbo has garnered top awards.
Left: Set your table with Cajun-inspired specialties: from left, Pecan-Rice Dressing, Baked Goose, and Brandied Sweet Potatoes.

91

LOUISIANA SEAFOOD GUMBO

    2 pounds unpeeled fresh shrimp
    7 cups water
    ¾ cup vegetable oil
    ¾ cup all-purpose flour
    3 cups chopped onion
    2 cups chopped green onions with
        tops, divided
    2 cups chopped celery
    1 cup chopped green pepper
    8 cloves garlic, minced
    3 bay leaves
    1 tablespoon salt
    ½ teaspoon red pepper
    ⅛ teaspoon garlic powder
    1 pound fresh lump crabmeat,
        flaked
    1 (12-ounce) container Select
        oysters, undrained
      Hot cooked rice
      Gumbo filé (optional)

Peel and devein shrimp, reserving shells; set shrimp aside. Combine shells and 7 cups water in a large saucepan; bring to a boil. Reduce heat and simmer, uncovered, 25 minutes. Strain shrimp stock, and set aside.

Heat oil in a large Dutch oven. Add flour, and cook over medium-high heat, stirring constantly, about 8 minutes or until mixture turns the color of a copper penny. Stir in onion, 1¾ cups green onions, celery, green pepper, and garlic. Cook over medium heat, stirring frequently, 10 minutes. Gradually add shrimp stock, stirring constantly. Add bay leaves, salt, red pepper, and garlic powder; bring mixture to a boil. Reduce heat and simmer, uncovered, 45 minutes.

Stir in shrimp, crabmeat, and oysters; simmer 6 to 8 minutes, or until seafood is done. Serve over rice in soup bowls. Add a small amount of gumbo filé to each serving, if desired. Garnish with remaining ¼ cup chopped green onions. Yield: 13 cups.

BAKED GOOSE

    1 (8- to 10-pound) goose
    ½ teaspoon salt
    ½ teaspoon pepper
    ½ teaspoon garlic powder
    3 slices bacon, cut into ½-inch
        pieces
    6 cloves garlic, chopped
    1 medium onion, quartered
    1 stalk celery, quartered
    2 large apples, unpeeled and cut
        into wedges
    2 (6-ounce) cans mushroom steak
        sauce
    2 cups chopped onion
    1 cup chopped celery
    1 cup sliced fresh mushrooms
    ½ cup chopped green pepper
    1 cup dry red wine
      Curly endive
      Grapes
      Kumquats

Remove excess fat from goose. Rinse goose thoroughly with cold water; pat dry.

Combine salt, pepper, and garlic powder; sprinkle ¼ teaspoon over surface and in cavity of goose. Cut pockets under meaty part of breast; stuff with seasoning mixture, bacon, and garlic. Stuff quartered onion, celery, and apples into cavity of goose, and close cavity with skewers. Tie ends of legs to tail with cord; lift wing tips up and over back so they are tucked under bird securely. Place goose in a roasting pan, breast side up. Insert meat thermometer in breast or meaty part of thigh, making sure it does not touch the bone.

Combine steak sauce and next 5 ingredients; pour into roasting pan. Cover and bake at 350° for 1 hour. Uncover and bake until thermometer registers 185° (about 2 to 2½ additional hours); baste goose frequently with sauce mixture.

Transfer goose to serving platter. Let stand 15 minutes before serving. Garnish platter with endive, grapes, and kumquats. Yield: 8 servings.

PECAN-RICE DRESSING

1 (12-ounce) container Standard
    oysters
¼ cup butter or margarine
1 bunch green onions, chopped
1 cup chopped celery
1 cup chopped onion
½ cup chopped green pepper
5 cloves garlic, minced
1 pound ground pork
½ pound ground beef
1¼ pounds chicken livers, chopped
1½ cups uncooked regular rice
3⅓ cups chicken broth
½ teaspoon salt
½ teaspoon pepper
½ cup chopped pecans, toasted
    Fresh parsley sprigs
1 cherry tomato

Drain oysters, reserving liquid; set aside.

Melt butter in a Dutch oven. Add green onions, celery, onion, green pepper, and garlic; cook over medium heat until tender, stirring occasionally. Remove from Dutch oven, and set aside.

Add pork and beef to Dutch oven; cook 5 minutes, stirring to crumble. Add livers; cook until no longer pink; drain well and return to Dutch oven.

Add sautéed vegetables, rice, broth, oyster liquid, salt, and pepper to meat mixture; cover and cook over medium heat 25 minutes. Add oysters; cook an additional 5 minutes. Remove from heat; stir in pecans. Garnish with parsley and cherry tomato cut like a daisy. Yield: 8 to 10 servings.

SHRIMP-STUFFED MIRLITONS

4 mirlitons (2½ to 3 pounds)
1 cup chopped onion
½ cup chopped celery
1 clove garlic, minced
2 tablespoons vegetable oil
¾ pound shrimp, peeled, deveined,
    and chopped
½ cup Italian seasoned breadcrumbs
2 eggs, beaten
¼ cup chopped fresh parsley
½ teaspoon salt
⅛ teaspoon pepper
    Celery tops
8 cooked, peeled shrimp (optional)

Wash mirlitons; slice lengthwise and place in a Dutch oven. Cover with water, and bring to a boil. Reduce heat and simmer 20 minutes or until tender. Drain and cool slightly. Discard seeds; scoop out pulp, leaving a shell. Chop pulp, and set aside.

Sauté onion, celery, and garlic in oil. Add chopped mirliton, and cook 10 minutes. Add ¾ pound shrimp and next 5 ingredients, and cook 8 minutes, stirring occasionally. Place mirliton shells in a 13- x 9- x 2-inch baking dish. Spoon shrimp mixture into shells. Bake at 350° for 15 minutes or until heated. Garnish with celery and cooked shrimp. Yield: 8 servings.

In south Louisiana, mirlitons, or chayote squash, are a staple; stuffed with shrimp, they're a delight. During the Christmas season, these unusual members of the gourd family are available in many well-stocked Southern grocery produce departments.

Floating Island Custard smoothly completes the feast. Try it alone or over a slice of pound cake.

BRANDIED SWEET POTATOES

  6 **large sweet potatoes**
½ **cup sugar**
  1 **tablespoon cornstarch**
½ **teaspoon salt**
½ **teaspoon ground
    nutmeg**
  1 **cup water**
⅓ **cup brandy**
  1 **tablespoon lemon juice**
½ **cup chopped pecans**
  1 **to 1½ cups miniature
    marshmallows**

Cook sweet potatoes in boiling salted water 25 minutes or until tender. Let cool to touch; peel and cut crosswise into ½-inch slices. Arrange potatoes in a lightly greased 13- x 9- x 2-inch baking dish. Set aside.

Combine sugar, cornstarch, salt, and nutmeg in a saucepan; stir to blend. Gradually add water; cook over medium heat, stirring constantly, until mixture comes to a boil. Boil 1 minute. Add brandy and lemon juice; pour over sweet potatoes. Sprinkle with pecans. Bake at 375° for 25 minutes; sprinkle with marshmallows, and bake an additional 5 minutes. Yield: 8 to 10 servings.

FLOATING ISLAND CUSTARD

¾ **cup sugar**
1 **tablespoon plus 1 teaspoon**
    cornstarch
¼ **teaspoon salt**
4 **eggs, separated**
4 **cups milk**
1½ **teaspoons vanilla extract**
¼ **cup sugar**
    Boiling water
    Pound cake (optional)

Combine first 3 ingredients in a large heavy saucepan, stirring well. Beat egg yolks, and stir into sugar mixture; stir in milk. Cook mixture, stirring constantly, over medium heat 15 to 20 minutes, or until mixture thickens and coats a metal spoon. Pour mixture into a large bowl, and stir in vanilla. Let cool, then cover and chill for at least 8 hours.

Beat egg whites (at room temperature) until soft peaks form. Gradually add ¼ cup sugar, 1 tablespoon at a time, beating until stiff peaks form. Pour about 1 inch of boiling water into a 13- x 9- x 2-inch baking pan; drop meringue by ½-cupfuls onto water. Bake at 350° for 15 minutes. Place meringues over custard using a slotted spoon. Cover and chill until serving time. Serve custard and meringues plain or over pound cake, if desired. Yield: 8 servings.

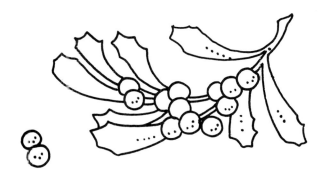

CAJUN PRALINES

2 **cups sugar**
1 **cup firmly packed brown sugar**
1 **cup milk**
½ **cup butter or margarine**
2 **tablespoons corn syrup**
4 **cups pecan halves**

Combine first 5 ingredients in a Dutch oven; bring to a boil. Cook, stirring constantly, until mixture reaches 225°. Add pecans and continue cooking, stirring constantly, until mixture reaches soft ball stage (236°). Remove from heat and beat vigorously with a wooden spoon until mixture just begins to thicken. Working rapidly, drop by tablespoonfuls onto greased waxed paper. Let stand until firm. Store in airtight container. Yield: 3½ dozen.

CAFÉ AU LAIT

4 **cups half-and-half**
4 **cups freshly brewed strong coffee**
    with chicory
    Sugar

Heat half-and-half in a saucepan just until bubbles form around edges of pan (do not boil). Pour coffee and half-and-half simultaneously into coffee cups or mugs. Sweeten to taste. Yield: 8 cups.

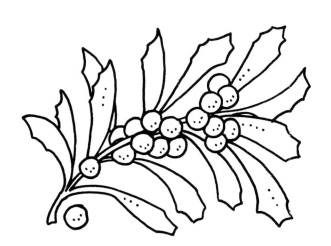

A Party for Tree Day

This year, schedule a family trip to a Christmas tree farm and choose from acres of the freshest trees available. Take a break to serve your search party hot soup, easily transported in a thermos. Once home, an informal supper of double-decker sandwiches keeps you out of the kitchen and in on the tree-trimming fun.

Take-Along Tomato Soup
Zippy Oyster Crackers
Hot Tea
Super Dagwood Sandwich
Fruit 'n' Crunch Salad
Gingerbread Cake Squares
Fireside Cranberry Tea
(Menu serves 6-8.)

TAKE-ALONG TOMATO SOUP

¼ cup minced onion
3 tablespoons butter or margarine, melted
3 tablespoons all-purpose flour
½ teaspoon salt
¼ teaspoon pepper
1 cup milk
4 cups tomato juice
1 small bay leaf
2 teaspoons chopped chives

Sauté onion in butter in a large saucepan until tender. Add flour, salt, and pepper, stirring until smooth. Cook 1 minute, stirring constantly. Gradually add milk and tomato juice; cook over medium heat, stirring constantly with wire whisk, until thickened. Add bay leaf; simmer 1 minute. Remove bay leaf. Stir in chives. Pour into an insulated container to transport. Yield: 5½ cups.

ZIPPY OYSTER CRACKERS

1 tablespoon butter or margarine
1 cup oyster crackers
¼ teaspoon seasoning salt

Melt butter in a skillet; add crackers, stirring to coat crackers. Sprinkle with seasoning blend. Let cool. Store in an airtight container. Yield: 1 cup.

Note: Celery salt or onion salt can be substituted for seasoning salt.

Left: At the Christmas tree farm, serve Take-Along Tomato Soup piping hot from an insulated container.

Opposite: After trimming the tree, settle back for a casual supper of Super Dagwood Sandwiches and Fruit 'n' Crunch Salad.

SUPER DAGWOOD SANDWICH

- 1 (14-ounce) loaf French bread
- 3 tablespoons butter or margarine, softened and divided
- ½ pound thinly sliced cooked ham
- 1 (6-ounce) package sliced provolone cheese
- 3 tablespoons Thousand Island dressing, divided
- ¼ pound thinly sliced turkey
- ¼ pound thinly sliced salami
- ¼ cup butter or margarine, melted
- 1 tablespoon sesame seeds, toasted

Slice bread horizontally into 3 equal layers using an electric or serrated knife. Spread first layer with 1½ tablespoons butter, and top with ham, cheese, and half of dressing. Top with second layer of bread. Spread second layer with 1½ tablespoons butter, and top with turkey, salami, remaining dressing, and third bread layer.

Combine ¼ cup butter and sesame seeds; brush on top and sides of loaf. Place loaf on baking sheet; bake, uncovered, at 400° for 15 to 20 minutes. Yield: 6 to 8 servings.

FRUIT 'N' CRUNCH SALAD

- 1 (8-ounce) can pineapple chunks, undrained
- ¼ cup plus 1 tablespoon mayonnaise or salad dressing
- 5 cups unpeeled, diced apple
- 1½ cups sliced carrot
- 1 cup sliced celery
- ¾ cup raisins
  Fresh parsley sprigs

Drain pineapple, reserving ¼ cup juice; set pineapple aside.

Combine reserved pineapple juice and mayonnaise; stir well, and set aside.

Combine pineapple with remaining fruit and vegetables. Pour dressing over fruit mixture, tossing gently. Chill at least 30 minutes. Garnish with parsley. Yield: 8 servings.

FIRESIDE CRANBERRY TEA

- 1 cup fresh cranberries
- 6 cups water, divided
- ⅔ cup sugar
- 2½ tablespoons cinnamon-flavored candies
- 2 whole cloves
- ⅓ cup orange juice
- 2 tablespoons lemon juice

Combine cranberries and 1⅓ cups water in a Dutch oven; bring to a boil. Cover, reduce heat, and simmer 6 minutes or until cranberry skins pop. Strain cranberries, discarding pulp and returning juice to Dutch oven.

Combine sugar, candy, cloves, and 1⅓ cups water; cook over low heat until melted. Add candy mixture to cranberry liquid; stir in juice and 3⅓ cups water. Heat thoroughly. Remove cloves. Yield: 6½ cups.

GINGERBREAD CAKE SQUARES

- ⅓ cup butter or margarine, softened
- ½ cup sugar
- 2 eggs, beaten
- ⅔ cup molasses
- 2 cups all-purpose flour
- 2 teaspoons baking powder
- ¼ teaspoon baking soda
- 2 teaspoons ground ginger
- 1 teaspoon ground cinnamon
- ½ teaspoon salt
- ¾ cup buttermilk
  Sweetened whipped cream

Cream butter; gradually add sugar, beating at medium speed until light and fluffy. Add eggs and molasses, beating well. Combine next 6 ingredients; add to creamed mixture alternately with buttermilk, beginning and ending with flour mixture. Mix well after each addition.

Pour batter into a greased and floured 9-inch square baking pan. Bake at 350° for 40 minutes. Cool and cut into squares. Top with whipped cream. Yield: 9 servings.

Breads

CINNAMON-SUGAR APPLESAUCE MUFFINS

½ cup butter or margarine, softened
¾ cup sugar, divided
2 eggs
¾ cup applesauce
1¾ cups all-purpose flour
2 teaspoons baking powder
½ teaspoon salt
¼ cup butter or margarine, melted
¼ teaspoon ground cinnamon

Cream ½ cup butter; gradually add ½ cup sugar, beating until light and fluffy. Add eggs, one at a time, beating well after each addition. Stir in applesauce. Combine flour, baking powder, and salt; add to creamed mixture, and stir just until moistened.

Spoon batter into greased 1¾-inch miniature muffin pans, filling half full. Bake at 425° for 15 minutes or until done. Remove from pan immediately, and brush muffin tops with melted butter. Combine remaining ¼ cup sugar and cinnamon; sprinkle sugar mixture over each muffin. Yield: 2½ dozen.

APPLE DANISH

Pastry (recipe follows)
1 cup sugar
2 tablespoons all-purpose flour
1 teaspoon ground cinnamon
6 cups peeled and thinly sliced apple
1 egg white, lightly beaten
1 teaspoon water
Glaze (recipe follows)

Divide pastry in half; roll out one half on waxed paper into a 15- x 10-inch rectangle. (Pastry will be thin.) Invert pastry into a buttered 15- x 10- x 1-inch jellyroll pan, and peel away waxed paper.

Combine sugar, flour, and cinnamon in a medium bowl. Add apples, tossing well; spoon onto prepared pastry.

Roll out remaining pastry on waxed paper into a 15- x 10-inch rectangle; invert pastry over filling, and peel away waxed paper. Make slits in several places to allow steam to escape. Seal and flute edges. Combine egg white and water; beat well and brush over pastry. Bake at 375° for 40 to 45 minutes or until golden brown. Drizzle glaze over pastry while warm. Cut into bars. Yield: 15 to 18 servings.

Pastry:

4½ cups all-purpose flour
1½ teaspoons salt
1½ cups shortening
2 egg yolks, beaten
½ to ¾ cup milk

Combine flour and salt; cut in shortening with pastry blender until mixture resembles coarse meal. Add egg yolks and sprinkle milk over surface; stir with a fork until dry ingredients are moistened. Shape into a ball; chill. Yield: pastry for one 15- x 10-inch danish.

Glaze:

1 cup sifted powdered sugar
2 tablespoons milk
1 teaspoon vanilla extract

Combine all ingredients, stirring well. Yield: about ½ cup.

GUMDROP WREATH BREAD

¾ cup milk
⅓ cup sugar
1 teaspoon salt
⅓ cup butter or margarine
1 package dry yeast
¼ cup warm water (105° to 115°)
3 eggs, well beaten
2 teaspoons grated lemon rind
5 to 5¼ cups all-purpose flour
¾ cup chopped gumdrops
½ cup chopped pecans
   Glaze (recipe follows)
   Gumdrop flowers (optional)

Combine milk, sugar, salt, and butter in a small saucepan; cook over low heat until butter melts. Cool the mixture to lukewarm (105° to 115°).

Dissolve yeast in warm water in a large mixing bowl. Let stand 5 minutes. Add milk mixture, eggs, and lemon rind; mix well. Add 2½ cups flour; beat at medium speed of an electric mixer about 2 minutes or until smooth. Stir in enough remaining flour to make a soft dough.

Turn dough out onto a lightly floured surface, and knead until smooth and elastic (about 1 minute). Place dough in a well-greased bowl; turn to grease the top. Cover and let dough rise in a warm place (85°), free from drafts, 1 hour or until the dough has doubled in bulk.

Punch dough down; turn dough out onto a lightly floured surface, and knead in chopped gumdrops and pecans.

Invert a well-greased 5-inch metal mixing bowl in center of a large greased baking sheet. Shape dough into 1½-inch balls and

---

Gumdrops scored diagonally and opened into little flowers garnish Gumdrop Wreath Bread. Chopped gumdrops and pecans throughout make this sweet bread a treat for breakfast or snacks.

place around mixing bowl, forming a circle; stack some balls to add dimension to loaf. Cover and let rise in a warm place, free from drafts, 1 hour or until doubled in bulk. Bake at 375° for 15 to 18 minutes or until lightly browned. Remove mixing bowl. Drizzle glaze over wreath while warm. Garnish with gumdrop flowers, if desired (see note). Yield: one round loaf.

Glaze:

1½ cups sifted powdered sugar
2 to 4 tablespoons milk
¼ teaspoon vanilla extract

Combine all ingredients, mixing well. Yield: about ⅔ cup.

Note: Make 12 to 15 gumdrop flowers for garnish, if desired. To make flowers, you'll need to flatten gumdrops on a surface sprinkled with granulated sugar. Then slice gumdrops as directed, and roll to ¹⁄₁₆-inch thickness on sugared surface; sprinkle gumdrops with extra sugar as needed to eliminate stickiness. Shape flattened gumdrops as directed below.

To make a rose, set a gumdrop upright on counter. Slice gumdrop into thirds vertically. Flatten each third into an oval as directed above. Roll the smallest piece into a cone, pinching at narrow end for stem. Roll remaining pieces around cone, pressing upper edges outward for a petal effect, and pinching at bottom for stem end. One gumdrop makes one rose.

To make a daisy, set a gumdrop upright on counter. Using kitchen shears or a sharp knife, cut 8 equally spaced slits through rounded top of gumdrop, not quite cutting to bottom; sprinkle cut surfaces with sugar as necessary to eliminate stickiness. Pick gumdrop up, and squeeze bottom together slightly to make petals open. From a gumdrop of contrasting color, shape a ¼-inch ball and press the ball gently into the center of the daisy. One gumdrop (plus 1 small gumdrop ball for the center) will make one daisy.

BUTTERSCOTCH BALLS

½ cup chopped pecans, divided
    (optional)
1 (32-ounce) package frozen bread
    dough, thawed
1 (3⅝-ounce) package butterscotch
    pudding mix
1 cup firmly packed brown sugar
½ cup butter or margarine, melted
2 tablespoons milk
1 teaspoon ground cinnamon

Sprinkle pecans into two greased 9-inch round cakepans.

Cut dough into 1-inch pieces, and arrange over pecans. Combine remaining ingredients; pour evenly over dough. Cover and let rise in a warm place (85°), free from drafts, 1 hour or until doubled in bulk. Bake at 350° for 20 to 25 minutes. Invert onto serving plates. Yield: two 9-inch coffee cakes.

ELEPHANT EARS

1 cup milk, scalded
2½ tablespoons sugar
1 tablespoon salt
2½ tablespoons shortening
1 package dry yeast
1 cup warm water (105° to 115°)
4½ cups all-purpose flour
    Vegetable oil
1 cup sugar
1 teaspoon ground cinnamon

Combine milk, 2½ tablespoons sugar, salt, and shortening, stirring until shortening melts; cool to 105° to 115°.

Dissolve yeast in warm water in a large mixing bowl; let stand 5 minutes. Add milk mixture and 2 cups flour to yeast mixture; stir until smooth. Gradually stir in enough remaining flour to make a soft dough.

Turn dough out onto a floured surface, and knead until smooth and elastic (about 8

to 10 minutes). Place in a well-greased bowl, turning to grease top. Cover and let rise in a warm place (85°), free from drafts, 1 hour or until doubled in bulk.

Punch dough down; turn out onto a lightly floured surface. Divide dough into 12 equal balls.

Heat 3 to 4 inches of oil to 375°. Roll each ball of dough into an oval, ⅛ inch thick. Carefully transfer one piece at a time to hot oil. Cook 3 to 5 minutes on each side or until golden brown. Drain on paper towels. Combine 1 cup sugar and cinnamon; sprinkle over warm pastries. Serve warm. Yield: 1 dozen.

BUTTERY YEAST ROLLS

1 package dry yeast
½ cup warm water (105° to 115°)
½ cup boiling water
½ cup butter or margarine
¼ cup sugar
1 teaspoon salt
1 egg, beaten
3½ cups all-purpose flour, divided
2 tablespoons butter or margarine,
    melted

Dissolve yeast in warm water; let stand 5 minutes. Combine boiling water, ½ cup butter, sugar, and salt in a large bowl; stir well. Cool to 105° to 115°. Add egg, 1 cup flour, and yeast mixture, mixing well. Gradually stir in enough remaining flour to make a soft dough; cover and chill 2 to 3 hours.

Turn dough out on a floured surface, and knead 4 or 5 times. Roll out to ¼-inch thickness; cut with a 2-inch biscuit cutter, and brush with melted butter.

Make a crease across each circle, and fold one half over. Gently press edges to seal. Place on greased baking sheets; bake at 375° for 12 to 15 minutes or until golden brown. Yield: 2 dozen.

Tie up a gift bundle of Herbed Breadsticks, flavored with oregano and basil. Or bake a basketful of Buttery Yeast Rolls, shaped like half-moons from folded circles of dough. One buttery bite and you'll crave another.

HERBED BREADSTICKS

- ¾ **cup boiling water**
- 2 **tablespoons shortening**
- 1 **tablespoon sugar**
- 1 **teaspoon salt**
- 1 **package dry yeast**
- 3 **cups all-purpose flour, divided**
- 1 **teaspoon dried whole oregano**
- 1 **teaspoon dried whole basil**
- 2 **egg whites**
- 3 **tablespoons butter or margarine, melted**

Combine water, shortening, sugar, and salt; stir until shortening melts. Cool to 105° to 115°. Add yeast to mixture; let stand 5 minutes. Stir in 1½ cups flour and herbs. Set mixture aside.

Beat egg whites (at room temperature) until soft peaks form; fold into flour mixture. Stir in enough remaining flour to make a stiff dough. Turn dough out on a floured surface, and knead until smooth and elastic (about 2 to 3 minutes). Place dough in a well-greased bowl, turning to grease the top. Cover and let dough rise in a warm place (85°), free from drafts, 1 hour or until the dough has doubled in bulk.

Punch dough down, and divide in half. Roll out half of dough on a floured surface to ¼-inch thickness. Cut into 5½- x ½-inch strips. Roll strips with both hands into 7-inch ropes. Place on ungreased baking sheets, and brush dough with butter. Bake at 400° for 12 minutes or until lightly browned. Repeat with remaining dough. Yield: 3 dozen.

Beverages

RUM-BRANDY-CHAMPAGNE PUNCH

1 cup boiling water
2 regular tea bags
½ cup sugar
½ cup lemon juice
½ cup peach brandy
½ cup rum
1 (28-ounce) bottle ginger ale, chilled
1 (25.4-ounce) bottle champagne, chilled
Ice ring or cubes

Pour boiling water over tea bags; cover, and let stand 5 minutes. Remove tea bags; add sugar, stirring until dissolved. Stir in lemon juice, peach brandy, and rum.

Combine tea mixture, ginger ale, and champagne in punch bowl; add ice ring. Yield: 10 cups.

Keep Hot Fruit Toddy on hand to warm up unexpected guests or carolers.

RED WINE PUNCH

1 (6-ounce) can frozen orange juice concentrate, thawed and undiluted
⅔ cup water
1 tablespoon powdered sugar
1 tablespoon lemon juice
2 cups Burgundy or other dry red wine
1 quart ginger ale, chilled

Combine first 5 ingredients, and chill thoroughly. Stir in ginger ale just before serving. Yield: 7 cups.

HOT FRUIT TODDY

1 (48-ounce) bottle cranberry juice cocktail
2 cups apple juice
1 teaspoon whole cloves
2 (3-inch) sticks cinnamon
2 cups orange juice
1½ cups rum
Additional cinnamon sticks

Combine cranberry juice, apple juice, cloves, and 2 cinnamon sticks in a large Dutch oven. Bring to a boil; reduce heat, and simmer 15 minutes. Discard spices. Stir in orange juice and rum, and cook until thoroughly heated. Serve with cinnamon stick stirrers. Yield: 10 cups.

SPIRITED EGGNOG

6 eggs
1½ cups Irish Cream liqueur
3 tablespoons to ⅓ cup whisky
¾ cup milk
3 cups crushed ice
½ cup whipping cream, whipped
Ground nutmeg

Place first 4 ingredients in container of an electric blender; process until well blended. Add ice; process on low speed until frothy. Pour into individual glasses; top with a dollop of whipped cream. Sprinkle with nutmeg. Yield: about 6 cups.

KAHLÚA COFFEE

6 cups hot coffee
¾ cup chocolate syrup
¼ cup Kahlúa or other coffee-flavored liqueur
¼ teaspoon almond extract
½ cup whipping cream, whipped

Combine coffee, chocolate syrup, Kahlúa, and almond extract in a large container; stir well. Serve immediately, topping each serving with a dollop of whipped cream. Yield: 7 cups.

NOT-SO-SWEET COFFEE PUNCH

½ cup instant coffee granules
6 cups boiling water
4 cups water
1 quart chocolate ice cream, softened
1 quart vanilla ice cream, softened

Dissolve coffee granules in boiling water. Add remaining 4 cups water. Add ice cream just before serving, stirring gently. Yield: 3 quarts.

CINNAMON HOT CHOCOLATE

1 (6-ounce) package semisweet chocolate morsels
½ cup sugar
⅓ cup water
¼ teaspoon ground cinnamon
1 cup whipping cream
Hot milk

Combine first 4 ingredients in a heavy saucepan. Cook over low heat, stirring frequently, until chocolate melts and mixture is well blended. Remove from heat; let cool slightly.

Beat whipping cream in a mixing bowl until soft peaks form; fold into chocolate mixture. This mixture may be stored in an airtight container in the refrigerator for several days.

To serve, spoon 1 heaping tablespoon chocolate mixture into individual mugs. Add about ¾ cup hot milk to each mug, stirring until blended. Yield: 3 cups mix.

Note: Chocolate mixture can be frozen in 1-tablespoon portions in ice cube trays.

SANTA'S PUNCH

6 (12-ounce) cans lemon-lime carbonated beverage, chilled
Maraschino cherries
1 (46-ounce) can pineapple juice, chilled
2 (6-ounce) cans frozen orange juice concentrate, thawed and undiluted
½ to 1 teaspoon peppermint extract

Fill 2 ice cube trays with lemon-lime carbonated beverage, reserving rest of the lemon-lime beverage. Place a cherry in each ice cube section. Freeze.

To serve, combine pineapple juice, orange juice, and peppermint extract. Slowly pour in remaining lemon-lime beverage. Add cherry-filled ice cubes. Yield: 15 cups.

Cakes and Pies

WHITE CHOCOLATE CAKE

¼ pound white chocolate, coarsely
    chopped
½ cup boiling water
1 cup butter or margarine,
    softened
2 cups sugar
4 eggs, separated
1 teaspoon vanilla extract
2½ cups sifted cake flour
1 teaspoon baking soda
1 cup buttermilk
    Coconut-Pecan Frosting

Combine chocolate and water, stirring until chocolate melts; set aside.

Cream butter; gradually add sugar, beating well at medium speed of an electric mixer. Add egg yolks, one at a time, beating well after each addition. Stir in white chocolate mixture and vanilla.

Combine flour and soda; add to chocolate mixture alternately with buttermilk, beginning and ending with flour mixture. Beat egg whites (at room temperature) until stiff peaks form; fold into chocolate mixture. Pour into 3 well-greased and floured 9-inch round cakepans. Bake at 350° for 25 minutes or until a wooden pick inserted in center comes out clean. Cool in pans 10 minutes; remove from pans, and cool completely on wire racks. Spread Coconut-Pecan Frosting between layers and on top and sides of cake. Yield: one 3-layer cake.

Coconut-Pecan Frosting:

1 cup evaporated milk
1½ cups sugar
¼ cup plus 2 tablespoons butter or
    margarine
4 egg yolks
1½ cups flaked coconut
1½ cups chopped pecans
1½ teaspoons vanilla extract

Combine milk, sugar, butter, and egg yolks in a heavy saucepan; bring to a boil and cook over medium heat 12 minutes, stirring constantly. Add coconut, pecans, and vanilla; stir until frosting is cool and of spreading consistency. Yield: enough for one 3-layer cake.

BLACK FOREST CAKE

½ cup butter or margarine, softened
1¼ cups sugar
2 eggs
2 cups sifted cake flour
⅓ cup cocoa
1 teaspoon baking soda
½ teaspoon salt
1 cup water
1 teaspoon almond extract
3 (3-ounce) packages cream cheese,
    softened
2 cups sifted powdered sugar
2 (12-ounce) cartons frozen whipped
    topping, thawed
2 cups canned cherry pie filling
    Toasted sliced almonds

Cream butter; gradually add sugar, beating well at medium speed of an electric mixer. Add eggs, one at a time, beating well after each addition.

Combine flour, cocoa, soda, and salt; add to creamed mixture alternately with water, beginning and ending with flour mixture. Mix well after each addition. Stir in almond extract.

Pour batter into 2 greased and floured 8-inch round cakepans. Bake at 350° for 20 to 25 minutes or until a wooden pick inserted in center comes out clean. Cool in pans 10 minutes; remove layers from pans, and let cool completely. Split layers horizontally; set aside.

Combine cream cheese and powdered sugar; beat until smooth. Fold in whipped topping.

Cherry topping and piped frosting veil the four chocolate layers of Black Forest Cake. Just one slice, though, and the delicious secret is revealed.

Place bottom half of one cake layer on cake plate; spread with about 1 cup cream cheese mixture. Place top half of layer over mixture; spread with half the pie filling. Place bottom half of second cake layer over pie filling; spread with about 1 cup cream cheese mixture. Place remaining top half of second layer over mixture. Pipe sides with remaining cream cheese mixture using a decorating bag fitted with large metal tip No. 5; pipe a border of cream cheese mixture around top of cake. Fill center with remaining pie filling; garnish with almonds. Yield: one 8-inch cake.

Peanut Brittle Cheesecake presents a delightful twist on an old favorite. Top it with piped whipped cream, crushed brittle, and a cherry.

PEANUT BRITTLE CHEESECAKE

1½ cups graham cracker crumbs
⅓ cup finely crushed peanut brittle
⅓ cup butter or margarine, melted
3 (8-ounce) packages cream cheese, softened
5 eggs, beaten
1 cup sugar
1 tablespoon grated orange rind
1 teaspoon vanilla extract
½ cup whipping cream, whipped
2 tablespoons finely crushed peanut brittle
1 maraschino cherry

Combine cracker crumbs, ⅓ cup crushed peanut brittle, and butter; mix well. Press mixture firmly on bottom and sides of a buttered 8-inch springform pan; set aside.

Beat cream cheese until light and fluffy; add eggs, sugar, orange rind, and vanilla. Beat until smooth. Pour into prepared crust; bake at 300° for 1 hour and 15 to 20 minutes or until set. Remove from oven; let cool. Cover and chill 8 hours or overnight. Just before serving, pipe whipped cream around edge using a decorating bag fitted with large metal tip No. 5. Sprinkle remaining 2 tablespoons crushed peanut brittle over whipped cream. Top with cherry. Yield: one 8-inch cheesecake.

MINCEMEAT-ICE CREAM CAKE

1 (16-ounce) frozen pound cake,
   thawed
1 cup commercial mincemeat
½ cup slivered almonds, toasted
1 teaspoon grated orange rind
1 quart vanilla ice cream, softened
1 cup whipping cream
¼ cup sifted powdered sugar
   Additional slivered almonds,
     toasted (optional)
   Maraschino cherries (optional)

Cut pound cake horizontally into 3 equal layers; set aside.

Fold mincemeat, ½ cup almonds, and orange rind into ice cream. Spread ice cream mixture between layers; cover and freeze 8 hours or overnight.

Beat whipping cream until foamy; gradually add powdered sugar, beating until soft peaks form. Frost top and sides of cake with whipped cream. Garnish with additional slivered almonds and cherries, if desired. Yield: 8 servings.

CARAMEL APPLESAUCE CAKE

½ cup butter or margarine, softened
1½ cups sugar
3 eggs
2 cups all-purpose flour, divided
2 teaspoons baking soda
   Pinch of salt
1 teaspoon ground cinnamon
½ teaspoon ground cloves
1½ cups applesauce
½ cup chopped dates
½ cup chopped pecans
   Fruit-Nut Filling
   Caramel Frosting

Cream butter; gradually add sugar, beating well at medium speed of an electric mixer. Add eggs, one at a time, beating well after each addition.

Combine 1¾ cups flour, soda, salt, cinnamon, and cloves; add to creamed mixture alternately with applesauce, beginning and ending with flour mixture. Mix well after each addition. Coat dates and pecans with remaining ¼ cup flour; fold into batter.

Pour batter into 3 greased and floured 8-inch round cakepans. Bake at 350° for 25 to 30 minutes or until a wooden pick inserted in center comes out clean. Cool in pans 10 minutes; remove layers from pans, and let cool completely.

Spread Fruit-Nut Filling between layers. Frost top and sides with Caramel Frosting. Yield: one 3-layer cake.

Fruit-Nut Filling:

¼ cup all-purpose flour
2 tablespoons sugar
½ cup water
¼ cup butter or margarine
¼ cup plus 2 tablespoons chopped
   dates
¼ cup plus 2 tablespoons raisins
¼ cup chopped pecans

Combine flour and sugar in a medium saucepan; stir well. Gradually stir in water. Add remaining ingredients, and cook over medium heat until thickened, stirring constantly. Cool. Yield: about 1½ cups.

Caramel Frosting:

1 cup butter or margarine
1 cup sugar
1 cup firmly packed brown sugar
1 cup evaporated milk

Melt butter in a heavy saucepan over medium heat; add sugar and milk. Cook over medium heat, stirring, to soft ball stage (236°). Remove from heat; cool 10 minutes.

Beat at medium speed of an electric mixer 8 to 10 minutes or until thick enough to spread. Spread immediately on cooled cake. Yield: enough for top and sides of one 3-layer cake.

AMARETTO CHOCOLATE CREAM PIE

  1 cup sugar
  ⅓ cup cornstarch
  ¼ teaspoon salt
  4 egg yolks
  2¾ cups plus 2 tablespoons milk
  2 (1-ounce) squares unsweetened
      chocolate, chopped
  ¼ cup amaretto
  2 teaspoons vanilla extract
  1 9-inch baked pastry shell
  1 cup whipping cream
  1 tablespoon amaretto
  ¼ cup sifted powdered sugar
      Shaved chocolate (optional)

Combine sugar, cornstarch, salt, and egg yolks in a heavy saucepan; stir well. Gradually stir in milk; add chocolate. Cook over medium heat, stirring constantly, until chocolate melts and mixture is thickened and bubbly. Remove from heat; stir in ¼ cup amaretto and vanilla. Pour into pastry shell. Place a piece of plastic wrap directly on top of filling; chill 8 hours or overnight.

Combine whipping cream, 1 tablespoon amaretto, and powdered sugar; beat until soft peaks form. Spread over pie; garnish with shaved chocolate, if desired. Yield: one 9-inch pie.

CUSTARD PECAN PIE

  2 tablespoons chopped pecans
  1 unbaked 9-inch pastry shell
  3 eggs, separated
  1 cup sugar
  1 tablespoon cornstarch
  1 cup milk
  1 cup chopped pecans
  ¼ cup butter or margarine
  ½ teaspoon cream of tartar
  ¼ cup plus 2 tablespoons sugar

Sprinkle 2 tablespoons pecans in pastry shell; bake at 450° for 12 to 15 minutes. Cool.

Beat egg yolks in a large heavy saucepan; add 1 cup sugar, cornstarch, milk, and 1 cup pecans, stirring well. Cook over medium heat, stirring constantly, until thickened and bubbly. Remove from heat. Add butter; stir until melted. Pour hot filling into pastry shell.

Beat egg whites (at room temperature) and cream of tartar at high speed of an electric mixer 1 minute. Gradually add ¼ cup plus 2 tablespoons sugar, 1 tablespoon at a time, beating until stiff peaks form and sugar dissolves (2 to 4 minutes). Spread meringue over hot filling, sealing to the edge of the pastry. Bake at 350° for 12 to 15 minutes or until meringue is golden brown. Yield: one 9-inch pie.

PINEAPPLE CHEESE PIE

  1 (20-ounce) can crushed pineapple,
      undrained
  1 cup sugar
  2 tablespoons cornstarch
  1 unbaked 9½-inch deep-dish pastry
      shell
  1½ cups sugar
  ¼ cup all-purpose flour
  4 (3-ounce) packages cream cheese,
      softened
  2 tablespoons butter or margarine,
      softened
  3 eggs
  1 teaspoon vanilla extract

Combine first 3 ingredients in a heavy saucepan; mix well. Cook over medium heat, stirring constantly, until thickened and bubbly; cool. Spoon into pastry shell; set aside.

Combine 1½ cups sugar and flour; mix well. Add remaining ingredients; beat until smooth. Pour over pineapple mixture; bake at 400° for 40 to 45 minutes or until browned and set. Cool; chill at least 3 hours. Yield: one 9½-inch pie.

Cut stars from cookie dough and place atop Cranberry Linzer Squares. After baking, cut the squares around the stars.

Cookies and Candies

CRANBERRY LINZER SQUARES

½ cup butter or margarine, softened
1 (8-ounce) can almond paste
1 cup sugar
2 eggs
½ teaspoon almond or vanilla extract
3¼ cups all-purpose flour
¼ teaspoon salt
1 (14-ounce) jar cranberry-orange sauce

Cream the butter and almond paste; add the sugar, eggs, and almond extract, beating well. Combine the flour and salt; then gradually add to the creamed mixture, mixing well. Measure and set aside 1½ cups of the almond mixture.

Spread remaining almond mixture in a lightly greased 15- x 10- x 1-inch jellyroll pan; top with cranberry-orange sauce, spreading evenly. Chill.

Roll reserved almond mixture between 2 sheets of waxed paper to ⅛-inch thickness. Place on a baking sheet; freeze 15 minutes. Remove the top piece of waxed paper, and cut the mixture with a 1½-inch canape cutter. Place the 54 cutouts over the cranberry mixture. Bake at 375° for 25 minutes or until lightly browned. Cool and cut into squares. Yield: 4½ dozen.

LUCKY STARS

¼ cup butter or margarine
¼ cup sugar
1 egg
1 teaspoon vanilla extract
⅛ teaspoon salt
1⅓ cups all-purpose flour
1½ teaspoons baking powder
Nut filling (recipe follows)

Cream butter and sugar; add egg, vanilla, and salt, beating well. Combine flour and baking powder; add to creamed mixture, stirring well.

Roll dough to ⅛-inch thickness on a floured surface. Cut with a 2½-inch star-shaped cookie cutter, and place on ungreased cookie sheets. Place a slightly rounded half-teaspoonful nut filling onto center of each star. Gently bring points of each star up and to the center; pinch points together so they stand upright, allowing filling to show through the sides.

Bake at 350° for 10 minutes or until lightly browned. Let cool slightly; remove cookies to wire racks, and cool completely. Yield: 4 dozen.

Nut Filling:

1¼ cups walnuts or pecans, finely chopped
⅓ cup sugar
2 tablespoons water
1 tablespoon butter or margarine, melted
⅛ teaspoon salt
⅛ teaspoon maple flavoring

Combine all ingredients; stir well. Yield: about 1 cup.

Sweeten the holidays with these special treats. On plate: Cranberry Linzer Squares and White Fudge. In cookie jar: Lucky Stars.

PEPPERMINT PATS

¾ cup butter or margarine, softened
¼ cup sugar
1 egg yolk
1 teaspoon vanilla extract
1 teaspoon peppermint flavoring
2 cups all-purpose flour
½ cup crushed hard peppermint candy
Sugar

Cream butter; gradually add sugar, beating until light and fluffy. Add egg yolk, beating well. Stir in flavorings. Gradually add flour; mix well. Stir in crushed candy. Shape mixture into 1-inch balls, and roll in sugar; place on ungreased cookie sheets. Bake at 350° for 15 minutes. Remove immediately from cookie sheets, and cool on wire racks. Yield: 4 dozen.

ORANGE MELTAWAYS

¾ cup butter or margarine, softened
½ cup sifted powdered sugar
1 tablespoon plus 1 teaspoon grated orange rind
1 teaspoon vanilla extract
1 cup all-purpose flour
½ cup cornstarch
2 tablespoons sugar

Cream butter; gradually add powdered sugar, beating until light and fluffy. Stir in orange rind and vanilla. Combine flour and cornstarch; add to creamed mixture, stirring well. Cover and chill 1 hour.

Divide dough in half; shape each half into a roll 5 inches long. Wrap in waxed paper, and then in aluminum foil; freeze 24 hours.

Roll dough in 2 tablespoons sugar. Cut dough into ¼-inch slices; place 1 inch apart on ungreased cookie sheets. Bake at 375° for 8 to 10 minutes. Cool on wire racks. Yield: about 3 dozen.

CHERRY-FILLED SUGAR COOKIES

½ cup shortening
1 cup sugar
1 egg
½ cup buttermilk
2½ cups all-purpose flour
1 teaspoon baking powder
½ teaspoon baking soda
   Pinch of salt
1 teaspoon vanilla extract
1 (10-ounce) jar cherry preserves

Cream shortening; gradually add sugar, beating until light and fluffy. Add egg and buttermilk, beating well.

Combine flour, baking powder, soda, and salt. Add to creamed mixture, beating well. Stir in vanilla.

Work with half of dough at a time; store remainder in refrigerator. Roll half of dough on a lightly floured surface to ⅛-inch thickness; cut into rounds with a 2½-inch cookie cutter. Roll remaining dough to ⅛-inch thickness; cut with a 2½-inch doughnut cutter. Place on lightly greased cookie sheets, and bake at 350° for 10 to 12 minutes or until lightly browned. Cool on wire racks.

Spread bottom side of solid cookies with cherry preserves, and top with bottom side of cut-out cookies. Yield: 4 dozen.

FAVORITE OATMEAL BARS

4 cups regular oats, uncooked
1 cup firmly packed brown sugar
¼ cup light corn syrup
⅔ cup butter or margarine, melted
¼ cup chunky peanut butter
1 teaspoon vanilla extract
1 (6-ounce) package semisweet
   chocolate morsels
½ cup butterscotch morsels
⅔ cup chunky peanut butter

Combine first 3 ingredients; add butter, ¼ cup peanut butter, and vanilla; stir well.

Spoon into an ungreased 13- x 9- x 2-inch baking pan. Bake at 400° for 12 minutes. Allow to cool.

Combine chocolate and butterscotch morsels in top of a double boiler; bring water to a boil. Add ⅔ cup peanut butter; reduce heat to low; cook, stirring, until melted and blended. Pour over baked mixture. Refrigerate until firm. Cut into bars. Store in refrigerator. Yield: 5 dozen.

MINCEMEAT BAR COOKIES

1½ cups firmly packed brown sugar
2 eggs
2 tablespoons molasses
1 tablespoon butter or margarine,
   softened
1 teaspoon vanilla extract
2 cups all-purpose flour
1 teaspoon ground cinnamon
1 teaspoon ground cloves
½ teaspoon baking soda
½ teaspoon salt
3 tablespoons hot water
1 (9-ounce) package mincemeat,
   crumbled
¼ cup sliced almonds
¼ cup raisins
1½ cups sifted powdered sugar
3 tablespoons milk
½ teaspoon almond extract
½ teaspoon vanilla extract

Combine brown sugar, eggs, molasses, butter, and 1 teaspoon vanilla extract, beating well at medium speed of an electric mixer. Combine flour, cinnamon, cloves, soda, and salt; add to egg mixture, mixing well. Stir in water, mincemeat, almonds, and raisins.

Spread mixture in a lightly greased 15- x 10- x 1-inch jellyroll pan. Bake at 350° for 12 to 15 minutes.

Combine remaining ingredients, stirring well. Pour mixture over baked layer, spreading evenly. Cool and cut into bars. Yield: about 5½ dozen.

CHOCOLATE-COVERED RAISINS

1 (6-ounce) package semisweet
    chocolate morsels
¼ cup dark corn syrup
2 tablespoons powdered sugar
1½ teaspoons vanilla extract
2 cups raisins

Combine chocolate morsels and corn syrup in top of a double boiler; bring water to a boil. Reduce heat to low; cook until chocolate melts, stirring constantly. Remove from heat, and stir in powdered sugar, vanilla, and raisins. Drop by half-teaspoonfuls onto waxed paper; chill. Store in refrigerator. Yield: about 5½ dozen.

CHOCOLATE-PEANUT CRUNCH

1 cup chunky peanut butter
1 tablespoon butter or margarine
½ teaspoon vanilla extract
⅛ teaspoon salt
1 cup sugar
⅓ cup light corn syrup
⅓ cup water
¾ pound chocolate almond bark

Combine first 4 ingredients in a heavy saucepan; bring to a boil. Reduce heat to low; cook until butter melts, stirring occasionally. Set aside.

Combine sugar, corn syrup, and water in a heavy saucepan. Cook over medium heat, stirring constantly, until sugar dissolves. Bring to a boil; cook, stirring, until mixture registers 305° on a candy thermometer.

Remove from heat; immediately add peanut butter mixture, stirring until blended. Working rapidly, spread mixture onto a buttered 15- x 10- x 1-inch jellyroll pan. Let cool.

Place chocolate in top of a double boiler; bring water to a boil. Reduce heat to low; cook until chocolate melts, stirring occasionally. Pour over candy; let cool. Break candy into pieces. Yield: about 1¾ pounds.

WHITE FUDGE

1⅓ cups sugar
⅔ cup non-dairy liquid coffee cream
½ cup butter or margarine
⅛ teaspoon salt
2 cups miniature marshmallows
½ pound white chocolate coating,
    finely chopped
1 tablespoon vanilla extract
    Red and green candied cherries
    (optional)

Combine sugar, cream, butter, and salt in a medium saucepan. Cook over medium heat, without stirring, until mixture reaches 240°.

Remove from heat, and add marshmallows, chocolate coating, and vanilla, stirring until marshmallows melt. Pour into a buttered 8-inch square pan. Cool and cut into diamonds. Garnish with candied cherries, if desired. Yield: 3 dozen.

PEANUT BUTTER DIVINITY

2½ cups sugar
½ cup light corn syrup
½ cup water
2 egg whites
½ cup chunky peanut butter

Combine sugar, corn syrup, and water in a 2-quart saucepan; cook over low heat, stirring constantly, until sugar dissolves. Cook over high heat, without stirring, until mixture reaches hard ball stage (260°).

Beat egg whites (at room temperature) at high speed of an electric mixer until stiff peaks form. Pour sugar mixture in a very thin stream over egg whites, while beating constantly at high speed. Continue beating 4 to 5 minutes until mixture holds its shape. Stir in peanut butter.

Quickly drop mixture by rounded teaspoonfuls onto waxed paper; cool. Yield: about 5½ dozen.

Gift Ideas

PIZZELLES

3 eggs
¾ cup sugar
¾ cup butter or margarine, softened
2 teaspoons anise seeds
1 teaspoon vanilla extract
1½ cups all-purpose flour
1 teaspoon baking powder
Vegetable oil

Beat eggs at medium speed of an electric mixer until foamy; gradually add sugar, beating until thick and lemon colored. Add butter, anise, and vanilla; mix well. Add flour and baking powder; beat until smooth.

Brush pizzelle iron lightly with oil; preheat iron over medium heat 2 minutes. Place 1 tablespoon batter in center of iron; close iron and cook 30 seconds on each side or until pizzelle is lightly browned. Repeat with remaining batter; cool on wire racks. Yield: 2½ dozen.

ORANGE RUM SAVARIN

1 package dry yeast
3 tablespoons sugar, divided
⅓ cup warm water (105° to 115°)
4 eggs, beaten
3 cups all-purpose flour, divided
⅛ teaspoon salt
⅔ cup butter or margarine, softened
⅓ cup finely chopped candied
     orange rind
Rum Syrup
¼ cup apricot preserves
Orange flower (optional)

Dissolve yeast and 1 teaspoon sugar in warm water in a large mixing bowl; let stand 10 minutes.

Add remaining 2 tablespoons plus 2 teaspoons sugar, eggs, 2 cups flour, and salt; beat at medium speed of an electric mixer 2 minutes. Add butter, 1 tablespoon at a time, beating well after each addition. Stir in the remaining 1 cup flour and the orange rind. Cover and let dough rise in a warm place (85°), free from drafts, 1 hour. (Batter will be very soft.)

Stir batter down; spoon evenly into a well-buttered 11-cup ovenproof ring mold. Cover and let rise in a warm place, free from drafts, 1 hour or until doubled in bulk. Bake at 375° for 35 minutes or until loaf sounds hollow when tapped. Remove loaf from pan, and place on a large platter; baste with hot Rum Syrup. Allow to sit until most of syrup is absorbed.

Melt preserves over low heat in a heavy saucepan. Spoon over bread. Garnish center of loaf with an orange flower, if desired. To make the orange flower, slice an orange into small wedges, cutting almost to, but not through, bottom. Place a rounded slice cut from an apple in the center of the flower. Yield: 12 to 15 servings.

Rum Syrup:

1 cup orange juice
¾ cup sugar
¼ cup plus 2 tablespoons light rum

Combine orange juice and sugar in a heavy saucepan; simmer 15 minutes. Remove mixture from heat; stir in rum. Yield: 1½ cups.

Orange Rum Savarin, a rich yeast cake soaked in Rum Syrup, will stay moist for several days when sealed in an airtight tin. Recipes for Pizzelles, lacy shapes cooked with a specialty iron, and salty Cracker Snackers yield enough for several gift packages.

CRACKER SNACKERS

- 1 (6-ounce) package Cheddar-flavored, tiny goldfish crackers
- 1 (6-ounce) package Parmesan-flavored, tiny goldfish crackers
- 1 (6-ounce) package plain tiny goldfish crackers
- 3 cups bite-size crispy wheat squares cereal
- 3 cups bite-size crispy corn squares cereal
- 2 cups corn-and-rice cereal
- 2 cups toasted oat cereal
- 8 to 10 cups walnut halves
- 2 tablespoons onion powder
- 2 tablespoons celery salt
- 1 tablespoon garlic powder
- 1 tablespoon pepper
- ½ cup butter or margarine, melted
- ½ cup bacon drippings, melted
- 2 tablespoons Worcestershire sauce
- 1 tablespoon hot sauce

Combine first 12 ingredients in a large container; toss well. Cover and let stand 8 hours or overnight.

Combine remaining ingredients; drizzle over cereal mixture, and toss well. Spread snack mixture onto three 15- x 10- x 1-inch jellyroll pans. Bake at 200° for 1 hour, stirring every 15 minutes. Let mixture cool completely, and store in airtight containers. Yield: 8 quarts.

SNAPPY BEER CHEESE

- 3 pounds sharp Cheddar cheese
- 2 small onions, quartered
- 3 tablespoons Worcestershire sauce
- 1½ tablespoons hot sauce
- 1 cup beer

Cut cheese into 1-inch chunks; spread out on paper towel-lined baking sheets, and let stand at room temperature 6 hours.

Position shredding disc in food processor bowl; top with cover. Place enough cheese in food chute to fill; shred cheese, applying pressure with food pusher. Shred remaining cheese; place in a large bowl, and set aside.

Position knife blade in processor bowl; add onions, and process until finely chopped. Combine onion and cheese; refrigerate, uncovered, at least 8 hours.

Let cheese mixture stand at room temperature about 1 hour; add Worcestershire sauce and hot sauce, mixing well. Cover and refrigerate 8 hours or overnight.

Pour beer over cheese mixture; let stand at room temperature about 1 hour.

Position knife blade in processor bowl; place about one-third of cheese mixture in processor bowl. Process until cheese is smooth, stopping to scrape sides of bowl occasionally. Repeat with remaining cheese mixture.

Pack cheese spread into gift containers. Store in refrigerator up to 3 weeks. Bring spread to room temperature before serving. Yield: 7 cups.

TAVERN BREAD

- ½ cup warm strong coffee (105° to 115°)
- 3 tablespoons molasses, divided
- 1 tablespoon honey
- 1 package dry yeast
- 1 (12-ounce) can evaporated milk
- 2 tablespoons regular oats, uncooked
- 2 tablespoons vegetable oil
- 2 teaspoons salt
- ¼ teaspoon ground ginger
- 3 cups all-purpose flour, divided
- 1½ cups whole wheat flour

Combine first 4 ingredients in a large mixing bowl; let stand 5 minutes. Add milk, oats, oil, salt, and ginger, stirring well. Stir in 1 cup all-purpose flour and 1½ cups whole wheat flour; beat at medium speed of an electric mixer 1 minute. Gradually add remaining 2 cups flour, stirring with a wooden spoon.

Spoon dough into 2 well-greased 1-pound coffee cans. Cover and let rise in a warm place (85°), free from drafts, 1 hour or until doubled in bulk.

Bake at 350° for 30 minutes. Remove bread from cans, and cool on wire racks. Yield: 2 loaves.

Note: Bread may also be baked in 2 well-greased 8½- x 4½- x 3-inch loafpans.

Dress up jar lids with paper doilies, for canned gifts like Herbed Green Olives and Cranberry Relish.

HERBED GREEN OLIVES

3 (16-ounce) jars cracked green olives in brine, drained
24 thin lemon slices
12 cloves garlic
2½ tablespoons dried whole thyme
1 tablespoon plus 1 teaspoon cracked peppercorns
8 bay leaves
Olive oil

Layer all ingredients except oil in four 1-pint jars. Pour oil into jars to barely cover olives. Cover and store at room temperature for 1 week before serving. Yield: 4 pints.

Note: If olives are kept longer than 2 weeks, store in refrigerator. Let come to room temperature before serving.

CRANBERRY RELISH

2 (16-ounce) cans whole berry cranberry sauce
2 tablespoons vinegar
2 teaspoons dry mustard

Combine all ingredients, stirring well. Store in refrigerator. Serve relish with poultry. Yield: 3⅓ cups.

SWEET AND SPICY NUTS

1½ cups pecan halves
1 cup whole almonds
1 cup walnut halves
1 cup hazelnuts
1 egg white
1½ tablespoons water
⅔ cup sugar
1 teaspoon salt
1 teaspoon ground cinnamon
1 teaspoon ground coriander
1 teaspoon ground ginger
¾ teaspoon ground allspice

Combine nuts in a large bowl; set aside.

Combine egg white and water in a medium mixing bowl; beat at high speed of an electric mixer until frothy. Stir in sugar, salt, and spices. Pour egg white mixture over nuts; toss until nuts are coated. Spread nut mixture onto a buttered 15- x 10- x 1-inch jellyroll pan. Bake at 275° for 55 minutes, stirring every 15 minutes. Let cool completely. Store in airtight containers. Yield: 6 cups.

Party Fare

LITTLE CRAB CREAM PUFFS

1 cup water
½ cup butter or margarine
1 cup all-purpose flour
¼ teaspoon salt
4 eggs
2 (7½-ounce) cans crabmeat, drained and flaked
1 cup (4 ounces) shredded Cheddar cheese
½ cup finely chopped celery
½ cup chopped ripe olives
½ cup mayonnaise
2 tablespoons finely chopped green onions
1 teaspoon grated lemon rind
Dash of garlic powder

Combine water and butter in a medium saucepan; bring mixture to a boil. Add flour and salt, all at once, stirring vigorously with a wooden spoon until mixture leaves sides of pan and forms a smooth ball. Remove from heat, and cool 4 to 5 minutes.

Add eggs, one at a time, beating thoroughly with a wooden spoon after each addition; then beat until batter is smooth.

Drop batter by teaspoonfuls onto lightly greased baking sheets. Bake at 425° for 10 minutes; reduce heat to 325°, and bake 8 to 10 minutes. Turn oven off; make a slit in puffs, and leave in oven 10 minutes to dry out. Remove cream puffs from oven, and cool on wire racks. Slice top third from each cream puff.

Combine remaining ingredients; mix well. Spoon 2 teaspoons crab mixture into each cream puff; replace tops. Place on ungreased baking sheets. Bake at 250° for 12 minutes.

To make ahead and bake later: fill the cream puffs; cover and chill them several hours or overnight. Bake them at 250° for 12 to 14 minutes or until thoroughly heated. Yield: 5 dozen.

STUFFED SHRIMP

6 cups water
2 pounds medium-size fresh shrimp
¼ cup crumbled blue cheese, softened
2 (3-ounce) packages cream cheese, softened
1 tablespoon mayonnaise
1 teaspoon paprika
1 teaspoon dried whole basil
1 teaspoon lemon juice
Lettuce
Cherry tomatoes

Bring water to a boil; add shrimp, and cook 3 to 5 minutes. Drain well; rinse with cold water. Chill. Peel and devein shrimp. Set aside.

Combine next 6 ingredients; mix well. Cut each shrimp in half lengthwise; spread about ½ teaspoon filling between halves. To serve, arrange on wooden picks on lettuce-covered craft-foam wreath, if desired. Arrange cherry tomatoes on wooden picks as garnish. Yield: about 7 dozen.

Create a tasty wreath of stuffed shrimp. Wooden picks anchor shrimp to a foam wreath, covered with greens, and clusters of cherry tomatoes add color.

CHERRY-SAUCED MEATBALLS

2 cups loosely packed torn bread
½ cup milk
1 tablespoon soy sauce
1 teaspoon garlic salt
¼ teaspoon onion powder
½ pound lean ground beef
½ pound hot bulk pork sausage
1 (8-ounce) can sliced water
    chestnuts, drained and chopped
    Cherry Sauce

Combine bread and milk; add soy sauce and seasonings, blending well. Combine beef and sausage, mixing well; add to bread mixture. Stir in water chestnuts. Shape into ¾-inch balls. Place on lightly greased rack of broiler pan; bake at 350° for 20 minutes. Place meatballs in chafing dish; pour Cherry Sauce over meatballs. Stir gently to coat and heat thoroughly. Serve in chafing dish with wooden picks. Yield: 4 dozen.

Cherry Sauce:

1 (21-ounce) can cherry pie filling
¼ cup vinegar
¼ cup steak sauce
⅓ cup dry sherry
2 tablespoons brown sugar
2 tablespoons soy sauce

Combine all ingredients in saucepan. Cook over medium heat until thoroughly heated. Yield: about 2½ cups.

PARTY CHEESE MOUSSE

1 envelope unflavored gelatin
¼ cup cold water
2 cups commercial sour cream
1 cup cream-style cottage cheese
¼ cup crumbled blue cheese
2½ teaspoons Italian salad dressing
    mix

Soften gelatin in cold water in a small saucepan. Cook over low heat, stirring constantly, until gelatin dissolves. Stir gelatin into sour cream. Add cottage cheese, blue cheese, and salad dressing mix; stir until blended. Spoon into a lightly oiled 3½-cup ring mold, and chill until set. Unmold just before serving. Yield: 16 appetizer servings.

CREAMY VEGETABLE-CHEESE DIP

1 (16-ounce) carton small-curd
    cottage cheese
1 (3-ounce) package cream cheese,
    softened
¼ cup finely chopped radishes
¼ cup finely chopped green onions
2 tablespoons chopped fresh parsley
1 clove garlic, crushed
¼ teaspoon salt
    Dash of pepper

Combine all ingredients in container of an electric blender; blend until smooth. Chill. Serve with fresh vegetables. Yield: about 2½ cups.

ITALIAN CHEESE CANAPÉS

2 cucumbers
1 (.07-ounce) package Italian
    dressing mix
1 (8-ounce) package cream cheese,
    softened
40 slices party rye bread
    Dried whole dillweed

Score cucumbers with the tines of a fork; cut into ⅛-inch slices. Set aside.
Combine dressing mix and cream cheese, mixing well. Spread about 1 tablespoon cream cheese mixture on each slice of rye bread. Top with a cucumber slice, and sprinkle with dillweed. Yield: 40 appetizers.

Serve Chocolate Fondue with fruit and cookies, such as Shortbread Pecan Fingers shown in foreground.

CHOCOLATE FONDUE

  1 (12-ounce) package semisweet
      chocolate morsels
½ cup half-and-half
½ cup sugar
  1 teaspoon vanilla extract

Combine all ingredients in top of a double boiler; bring water to a boil. Reduce heat to low, and cook over low heat until chocolate melts, stirring occasionally. Pour into fondue pot; place over fondue burner. Serve with assorted fruit or cookies as dippers. Yield: 2 cups.

MINI FRUIT CUPCAKES

½ pound red candied cherries,
     chopped
½ pound green candied cherries,
     chopped
  1 pound candied pineapple, chopped
  3 tablespoons Grand Marnier or
     other orange-flavored liqueur
  4 cups chopped pecans
  1 pound chopped dates
  3 eggs, beaten
¾ cup sugar
¾ cup self-rising flour

Combine first 3 ingredients in a large bowl. Pour liqueur over fruit; cover and marinate overnight.

Add pecans and dates to fruit mixture; stir well. Combine eggs and sugar; stir in flour. Stir egg mixture into fruit mixture, blending well.

Spoon 1 heaping tablespoon batter into well-greased 1¾-inch muffin pans. Bake at 300° for 30 minutes. Yield: about 7 dozen.

SHORTBREAD-PECAN FINGERS

½ cup butter or margarine, softened
  2 tablespoons powdered sugar
  1 cup self-rising flour
  1 teaspoon vanilla extract
  1 cup finely chopped pecans
    Sifted powdered sugar

Cream butter; add 2 tablespoons powdered sugar, and beat at medium speed of an electric mixer until light and fluffy. Add flour and vanilla; mix well. Fold in pecans. Shape dough into 1½- x ½-inch fingers; place on ungreased cookie sheets. Bake at 300° for 30 minutes or until lightly browned. Remove to wire racks and let cool 10 minutes; roll in additional powdered sugar. Place on wire racks to cool completely. Yield: 3 dozen.

Christmas Journal

Reflecting on past Christmases, we are likely to recall exchanging gifts, sending greetings to friends, embellishing our homes with greenery, and toasting and caroling in celebration of this international festival of faith and goodwill. To help with holiday preparations, the following pages are filled with solid advice on the finer points of planning for and enjoying the holidays, such as mailing information, size charts to insure a correct fit, and plenty of pages to keep track of Christmas cards, gifts, and wishes. Tips on taking memorable photographs, fire and electrical safety awareness, and choosing toys that will be safe for children emphasize the practical side of the Yuletide.

But how did all these customs develop? If some traditions are older than Christmas itself, what are the roots of our revelry? Many Christmas practices observed today developed through a symbiotic relationship between pagans and the Christian church, while other ancient Christmas beliefs have profound religious origins. The historical facts and glimpses offered here into the sources of today's treasured practices will heighten your appreciation of this celebration.

Christmas is a nostalgic time, and traditions are rich, lovely rituals in which we should indulge ourselves and share with others. Besides their historical importance, these time-honored ways give us a link to the past and the future—a belonging to something much larger than we are—by allowing us to be a part of an experience that mankind has cherished and repeated for hundreds of years. And each time we celebrate, our beliefs are passed to later generations. It is this mixture of custom, reverence, and charity that makes Christmas a masterpiece of imagination, beauty, and love.

Mailing

CARDS

Keep in mind the following U.S. Postal regulations. Envelopes must be rectangular in shape. Envelopes smaller than 3½" × 5" cannot be mailed. Envelopes larger than 6⅛" × 11½", even if they weigh less than 1 ounce, require extra postage.

PACKAGES

·Before you wrap a package, consider the contents, the sturdiness of the box, the cushioning, and closure with tape.

Choose a sturdy box. Include adequate cushioning. Place your return address and address of the recipient inside the box. Wrap the package in brown paper. Use a filament tape. Masking tape, cellophane tape and surgical tape are just not strong enough. Address clearly.

Packages may be sent through the U.S. Postal Service by parcel post in weights up to 70 pounds and measurements of 108" of combined length and girth.

United Parcel Service (UPS) accepts packages up to 50 pounds for delivery in state, 70 pounds in interstate shipment, and up to 108" in combined length and girth. There is a pick-up fee for door-to-door service.

CATEGORY	EXAMPLES	CONTAINER	CUSHIONING	CLOSURE
Soft Goods		Self-supporting box or tear-resistant bag		Reinforced tape or sealed bag
Liquids		Leak proof interior and secondary containers	Absorbent	Sealed with filament tape
Powders		Must be sift-proof		Sealed with filament tape
Perishables		Impermeable to content odor	Absorbent	Sealed with filament tape
Fragile Items		Fiberboard (minimum 175 lb test)	To distribute shocks and separate from container surfaces with foamed plastic or padding	Sealed and reinforced with filament tape
Awkward Loads		Fiberboard tubes and boxes with length not over 10 times girth	Pre-formed fiberboard or foamed plastic shapes	Tube ends equal to side wall strength

CONTAINER	CUSHIONING	CLOSURE	ADDRESSING
Fiberboard Manufacturer's Certificate 125 lb test to 20 lbs 175 lb test to 40 lbs 275 lb test to 70 lbs Paperboard up to 10 lbs	Wrap each item individually with enough padding to prevent damage from shock Separate wrapped items from outer package surfaces with padding or foamed plastic	Pressure Sensitive Filament Tape is preferable to prevent accidental opening Reinforced Kraft Paper Tape Kraft Paper Tape	Address Labels should be readable from 30" away and should not be easily smeared or washed off Should contain ZIP Code Return Address should also be included inside of carton

Adapted from a U.S. Postal Service poster.

Gifts & Wishes

Name		Name	
height	weight	height	weight
coat	slacks	coat	slacks
dress	pajamas	dress	pajamas
suit	bathrobe	suit	bathrobe
sweater	shoes	sweater	shoes
shirt	hat	shirt	hat
blouse	gloves	blouse	gloves
skirt	ring	skirt	ring

Name		Name	
height	weight	height	weight
coat	slacks	coat	slacks
dress	pajamas	dress	pajamas
suit	bathrobe	suit	bathrobe
sweater	shoes	sweater	shoes
shirt	hat	shirt	hat
blouse	gloves	blouse	gloves
skirt	ring	skirt	ring

Name		Name	
height	weight	height	weight
coat	slacks	coat	slacks
dress	pajamas	dress	pajamas
suit	bathrobe	suit	bathrobe
sweater	shoes	sweater	shoes
shirt	hat	shirt	hat
blouse	gloves	blouse	gloves
skirt	ring	skirt	ring

Name		Name	
height	weight	height	weight
coat	slacks	coat	slacks
dress	pajamas	dress	pajamas
suit	bathrobe	suit	bathrobe
sweater	shoes	sweater	shoes
shirt	hat	shirt	hat
blouse	gloves	blouse	gloves
skirt	ring	skirt	ring

Christmas Card List

CHRISTMAS CARD LIST (CONTINUED)

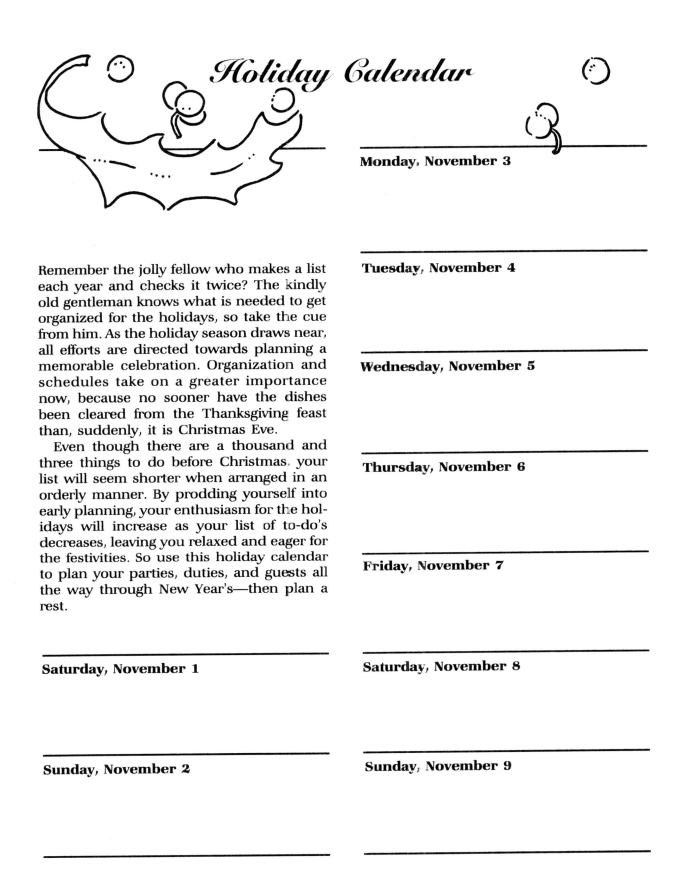

Holiday Calendar

Remember the jolly fellow who makes a list each year and checks it twice? The kindly old gentleman knows what is needed to get organized for the holidays, so take the cue from him. As the holiday season draws near, all efforts are directed towards planning a memorable celebration. Organization and schedules take on a greater importance now, because no sooner have the dishes been cleared from the Thanksgiving feast than, suddenly, it is Christmas Eve.

Even though there are a thousand and three things to do before Christmas, your list will seem shorter when arranged in an orderly manner. By prodding yourself into early planning, your enthusiasm for the holidays will increase as your list of to-do's decreases, leaving you relaxed and eager for the festivities. So use this holiday calendar to plan your parties, duties, and guests all the way through New Year's—then plan a rest.

Monday, November 3

Tuesday, November 4

Wednesday, November 5

Thursday, November 6

Friday, November 7

Saturday, November 8

Sunday, November 9

Saturday, November 1

Sunday, November 2

Monday, November 10

Monday, November 17

Tuesday, November 11

Tuesday, November 18

Wednesday, November 12

Wednesday, November 19

Thursday, November 13

Thursday, November 20

Friday, November 14

Friday, November 21

Saturday, November 15

Saturday, November 22

Sunday, November 16

Sunday, November 23

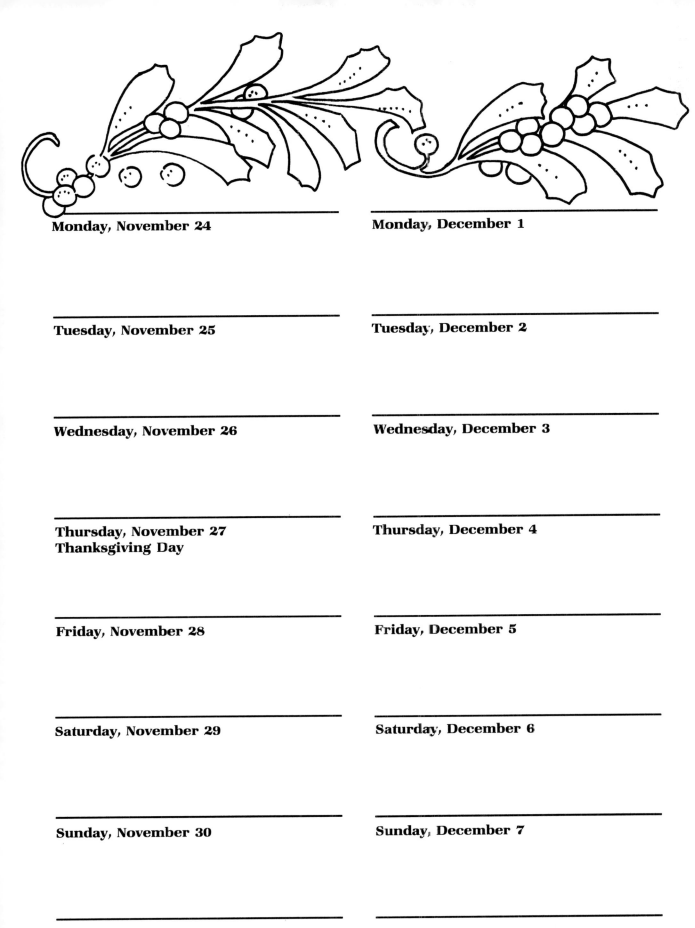

Monday, November 24

Tuesday, November 25

Wednesday, November 26

Thursday, November 27
Thanksgiving Day

Friday, November 28

Saturday, November 29

Sunday, November 30

Monday, December 1

Tuesday, December 2

Wednesday, December 3

Thursday, December 4

Friday, December 5

Saturday, December 6

Sunday, December 7

Monday, December 8

Monday, December 15

Tuesday, December 9

Tuesday, December 16

Wednesday, December 10

Wednesday, December 17

Thursday, December 11

Thursday, December 18

Friday, December 12

Friday, December 19

Saturday, December 13

Saturday, December 20

Sunday, December 14

Sunday, December 21

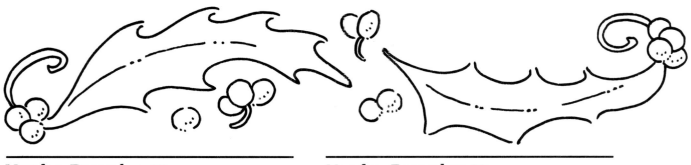

Monday, December 22

Monday, December 29

Tuesday, December 23

Tuesday, December 30

Wednesday, December 24

Wednesday, December 31

Thursday, December 25
Christmas Day

Thursday, January 1
New Year's Day

Friday, December 26

Saturday, December 27

Sunday, December 28

Yuletide Tips and Traditions

Legend and lore, fact and fancy—the strands of what Christmas has been, when woven together, flow into the fabric of Christmas now. Read on. Here, you'll wind through entertaining, informative, and useful glimpses of the most complex and exciting of holidays.

The Story of the Christmas Tree

Like lightning bugs emerging at dusk, first one window sparkles with Christmas tree lights, then a few more luminous trees appear, and after what seems no time at all, homes throughout the land blink and twinkle a sentimental exchange. The wonder of Christmas trees is a legacy from Germany.

Some say the tradition began in the 8th century. The Christian missionary St. Boniface led a group of German converts into the forest to chop down a sacred oak of the god Odin, and the felled tree uncovered a small fir. St. Boniface instructed his followers to take fir trees into their homes because the branches point toward heaven and the Christ Child.

Other legends credit Martin Luther, who was inspired by a stroll on a starry winter's night. He placed candles on an evergreen tree to create an allegory for his children, using the array of tiny flames to represent the stars in the sky over Bethlehem.

Make Trees as Safe as They Are Pretty

Dangle the ornaments, drape the tinsel, and do it with an eye towards safety. First, choose a Christmas tree that's very fresh, and keep it well-watered to reduce the risk of fire. When you unpack your lights, check them closely for fraying wires, loose connections, and damaged sockets. Join no more than three strands of lights, and be careful not to overload wall sockets. Attach lights so that the bulbs don't touch needles or branches, make sure cords lie clear of the tree's water reservoir, and turn off lights before you leave or go to bed.

If you have a young child in your home, hang breakable ornaments and those that could be swallowed, high out of reach, and always keep a close eye when a toddler is near the tree—pulling at ornaments or branches could topple the tree onto the child.

Flames from the Yule Log

In deep, dark, ancient Scandinavia, Norsemen thought of the year as a wheel. At the winter solstice, on December 22, they lit bonfires to celebrate the triumph of the sun over darkness. To fuel the raging fires, they used enormous pieces of wood. These logs became known as Yule logs, the word Yule coming from the Norse word for wheel.

Over the centuries, the custom endured and slowly evolved. In England, tradition dictated that the Yule log be lit on Christmas Eve and burned for a period each day until Twelfth Night. The charred remainder was then positioned under a bed to fight off fires, lightning, and evil spirits, until the following Christmas, when it became kindling for the new Yule log.

In some places today, the custom is enjoying a revival, again warmly marking the days of Christmas.

Carefully Light the Fires of Christmas

A flickering fire draws people together at Christmas, warming heart and soul. Be sure that's all it warms. Place your tree a safe distance from the fireplace, and use a screen to protect your room from popping sparks. Keep candles away from the tree and other flammable materials such as Christmas cards. Take care that candles aren't sitting where a child could grab them or pull them over by yanking a tablecloth, and snuff flames before they burn too low.

From St. Nicholas to Santa Claus

As the big visit approaches each year, children all across America become helpful around the house, kind to siblings and pets, and studious in the classroom. We all know who's responsible, but did you realize that Santa as we know him has only been around for a little over one hundred years? And that despite European beginnings, he's uniquely American?

A humorous tale by Washington Irving described the early Dutch settlers' fondness for Sinterklaas, or St. Nicholas. In Irving's story, the jolly old man is first described flying over rooftops and dropping presents down chimneys. In 1822, Clement Clarke Moore drew from this story when he penned his famous poem *A Visit from St. Nicholas*. And it was during the Civil War that Thomas Nast, a cartoonist for *Harper's Weekly*, gave Santa his now-famous and traditional appearance. He sketched the old gent with a round belly, dressed in fur-trimmed garb, and smoking a clay pipe.

Today's Santa, as he listens to children's wish lists and smiles with them for the camera, still looks the way Moore and Nast depicted him.

Develop Shutter Savvy

When you've carefully decorated your home in preparation for Santa, pictures are in order. Try these quick tips to capture the fun on film successfully. First, let the camera-shy celebrate in peace. If you encounter unwilling subjects, try taking your shots outside or in a designated room so that the occasion is comfortable for everyone.

If you do take pictures outside, arrange to do it in mid-morning or mid-afternoon when shadows are the softest. Get close to your subject. The people you're photographing should fill most of the viewfinder. Keep your shots uncluttered, and watch for objects that might appear to be growing out of your subjects' heads. Go for action shots. For toddlers and babies, use toys to divert their attention. If you're shooting video, film an event such as tree trimming, unwrapping the gifts, or singing carols around the piano. Then, when all is said and done, work out a reasonable and friendly way for everyone interested to get copies.

Greetings via Post

We can thank an inventive Englishman, the holiday rush, and the one-penny post for Christmas cards. In the 1840s, Sir Henry Cole found the task of writing personal greetings to all of his associates more than he could face. Partly inspired by the new inexpensive postal rates, he decided to commission an artist to create a scene that expressed his sentiments; then he added a message and had a thousand cards printed. Those he didn't use were sold through a local shop, and as he predicted, he wasn't the only person with too little time—the custom is now part of our culture.

Send Cards
With Noteworthy Postmarks

Add whimsy to your season's greetings this year. Send out cards postmarked in a city named Christmas, Mistletoe, Noel, or Rudolph. Address and stamp your cards early, box them up, mark "Postmark Request" on the outside of the box, and send them to the postmaster in one of these towns: Bethlehem, GA 30620; Bethlehem, KY 40007; Bethlehem, MD 21609; Bethlehem, NC 28601; Christmas, FL 32709; Christmas Lake Village, IN 47579; Mistletoe, KY 41351; Nazareth, KY 40048; Nazareth, TX 79063; Noel, MO 64854; North Pole, AK 99705; North Pole, CO 80809; North Pole, NY 12946; Rudolph, OH 43462; Rudolph, WI 54475; Santa Claus, IN 47579; Silver Bell, AZ 85653; Silver Star, MT 59751; Wiseman, AR 72587.

Toasts from the Wassail Bowl

In merry old England, revelers went from house to house spreading the cheer of the Christmas season. To all who bade them good welcome, they drank a toast from a bowl of steaming wassail, which was hot spiced ale topped with toasted apples. In fact, the term "toasting" probably came from the pieces of "toast" floating in the bowl. The sentiments of those roving merrymakers have been handed down to us in the famous English carol: "Love and joy come to you, and to you your wassail too, and God bless you and send you a Happy New Year, and God send you a Happy New Year."

Mix Wisdom with Spirits of the Season

The dangers of drinking and driving are fortunately receiving the public attention they deserve. Especially during the holidays, take every precaution to prevent your celebrations from resulting in tragedy. But also be aware of another alcohol-related danger. Every year there are reports of severe illness and even death among small children who've drunk from liquor bottles. Make sure your bottles are out of reach. You can't rely on the strong taste to repel inquisitive and imitative toddlers.

After Christmas, There's Boxing Day

In 19th-century England, local tradesmen called for their annual tips on the day after Christmas. The money was placed in small earthenware boxes that had to be broken to release their contents. As a result, December 26 became known as Boxing Day, and in many parts of the British Commonwealth, it is still a day of celebration.

Let Holiday Tips Say Thank You

A gift of crisp bills at Christmas gracefully thanks many of those who have performed valuable services through the year—people such as hairdressers, paper boys, gardeners, housekeepers, babysitters, and delivery boys. But how much to tip can be tricky, since tipping carries no formal rules. Customs vary from city to city, and each relationship is different.

Generally, the length of the relationship and your satisfaction with the service you've received should determine the size of your tip. If you tip throughout the year, you should increase the amount for the holidays. If you're extremely friendly with someone, you might choose to give a small gift rather than cash. If so, make sure it's appropriate—for example, a gift of wine to a non-drinker would fall short of expressing your sincere gratitude.

The First Christmas Gifts

Epiphany (a Greek word that means arrival) falls on January 6 and is the last of the 12 days of Christmas. This marks the day that the three Magi found the Christ Child in a stable in Bethlehem. As the Gospel of St. Matthew relates: "When they saw the star, they rejoiced with exceeding great joy. And when they were come into the house, they saw the young child with Mary his mother, and fell down, and worshipped him: and when they had opened their treasures, they presented unto him gifts; gold, and frankincense, and myrrh." Each present given at Christmastime today is an echo of those first, most-precious gifts.

Choose Fun and Safe Toys

Toys follow fashion and fad just like everything else. Luckily they've also followed the trend toward consumer awareness and safety. When buying toys for children, heed the age guidelines. Be especially careful about toys with small parts, projectiles, and sharp or pointed edges.

Check how well-made an item is—loose buttons can choke. Make sure painted toys are nontoxic, all fabrics are flame-resistant, and electrically operated toys are approved by Underwriters Laboratories Inc. (UL).

Patterns

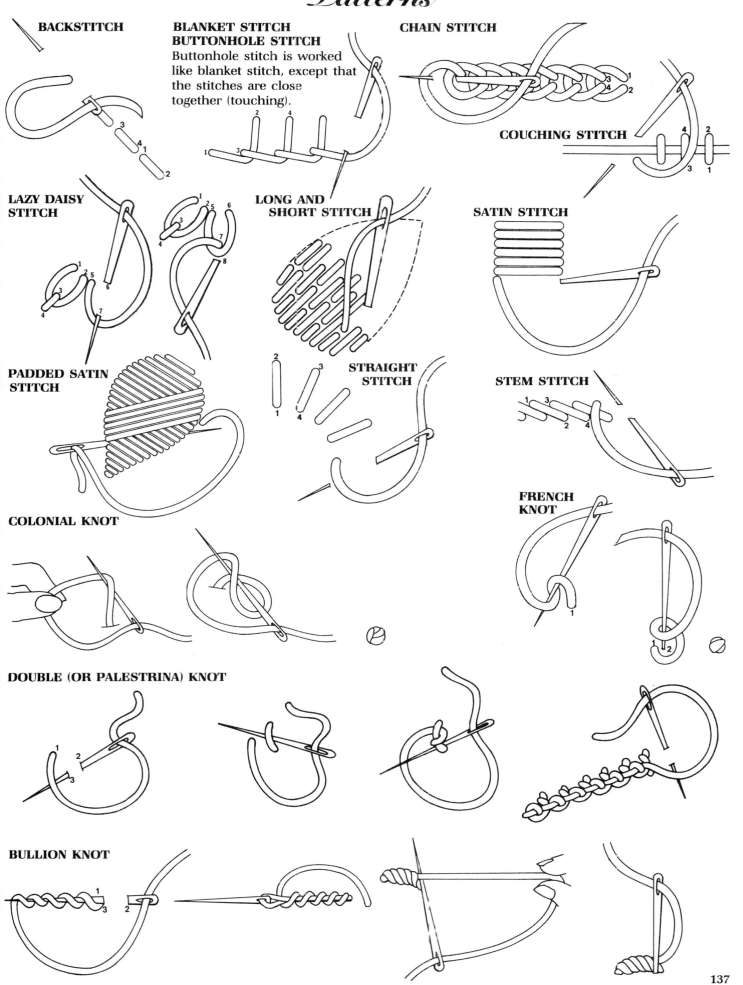

BACKSTITCH

BLANKET STITCH
BUTTONHOLE STITCH
Buttonhole stitch is worked like blanket stitch, except that the stitches are close together (touching).

CHAIN STITCH

COUCHING STITCH

LAZY DAISY STITCH

LONG AND SHORT STITCH

SATIN STITCH

PADDED SATIN STITCH

STRAIGHT STITCH

STEM STITCH

COLONIAL KNOT

FRENCH KNOT

DOUBLE (OR PALESTRINA) KNOT

BULLION KNOT

A Christmas Composition

**Instructions are on page 40.
Patterns are full-size.**

SHEET MUSIC ORNAMENTS

Punch hole
for hanger.

Punch hole
for hanger.

Punch hole
for hanger.

Punch hole
for hanger.

138

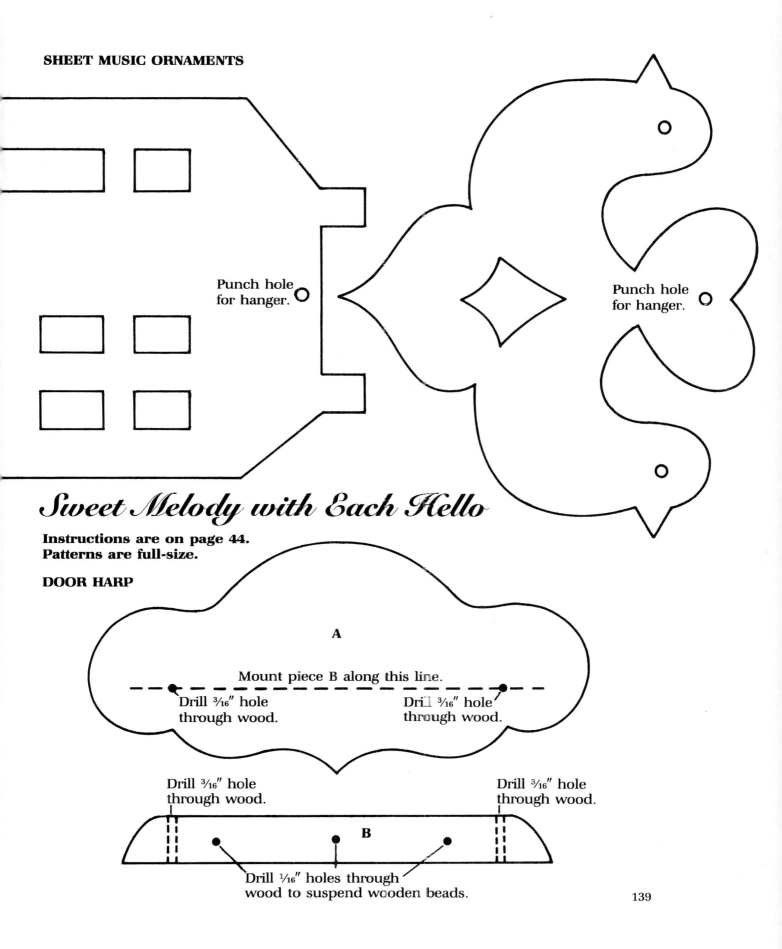

Punch hole
for hanger.

Punch hole
for hanger.

Sweet Melody with Each Hello

Instructions are on page 44.
Patterns are full-size.

DOOR HARP

A

Mount piece B along this line.

Drill 3/16" hole
through wood.

Drill 3/16" hole
through wood.

Drill 3/16" hole
through wood.

Drill 3/16" hole
through wood.

B

Drill 1/16" holes through
wood to suspend wooden beads.

139

Whitework: Understated Elegance

Instructions are on page 46.
Pattern is full-size.
Pattern includes ¼″ seam allowance
for stocking pieces, ⅛″ seam
allowance for lining pieces.
For Stitch Diagrams, see page 137.

140

Stitch Key
(Note: Stitch Diagrams
are on page 137.)

1—Padded Satin Stitch
2—Satin Stitch
3—French Knot
4—Backstitch
5—Double (or Palestrina) Knot
6—Buttonhole Stitch

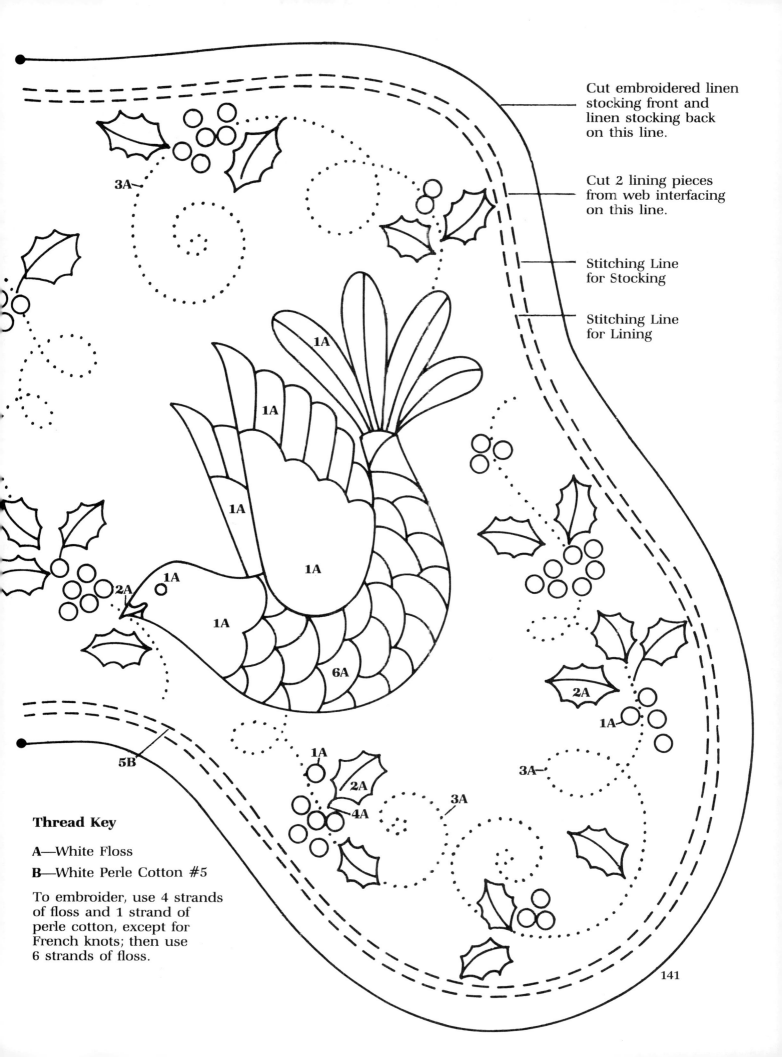

Cut embroidered linen stocking front and linen stocking back on this line.

Cut 2 lining pieces from web interfacing on this line.

Stitching Line for Stocking

Stitching Line for Lining

3A

2A

1A

1A

1A

1A

1A

1A

6A

2A

1A

3A

5B

1A

2A

4A

3A

Thread Key

A—White Floss

B—White Perle Cotton #5

To embroider, use 4 strands of floss and 1 strand of perle cotton, except for French knots; then use 6 strands of floss.

141

Add Punch to a Simple Box

Instructions are on page 82.
Pattern is full-size.

PUNCHED-COPPER FOIL BOX TOPPER

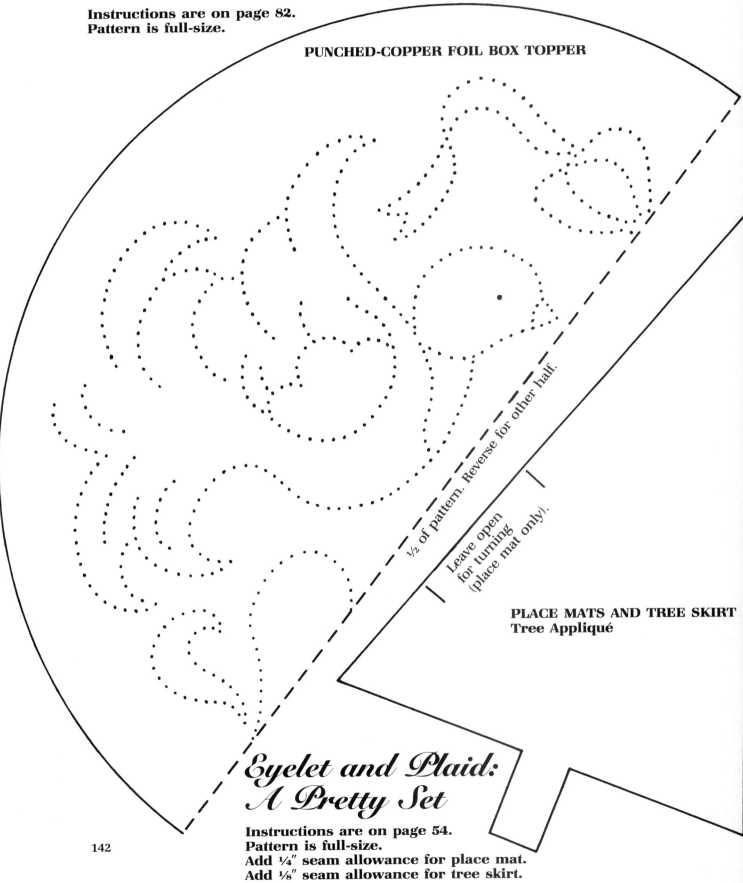

½ of pattern. Reverse for other half.

Leave open
for turning
(place mat only).

PLACE MATS AND TREE SKIRT
Tree Appliqué

Eyelet and Plaid: A Pretty Set

Instructions are on page 54.
Pattern is full-size.
Add ¼" seam allowance for place mat.
Add ⅛" seam allowance for tree skirt.

Tucked Away for a Merry Day

Instructions are on page 50.
Patterns are full-size.
Patterns include ¼″ seam allowance.

Diagram—Making Tucks

Machine-Stitched Line

Right Side of Fabric

Fold fabric and stitch in place for desired tuck width.

Distance between tucks should be at least the width of the tuck.

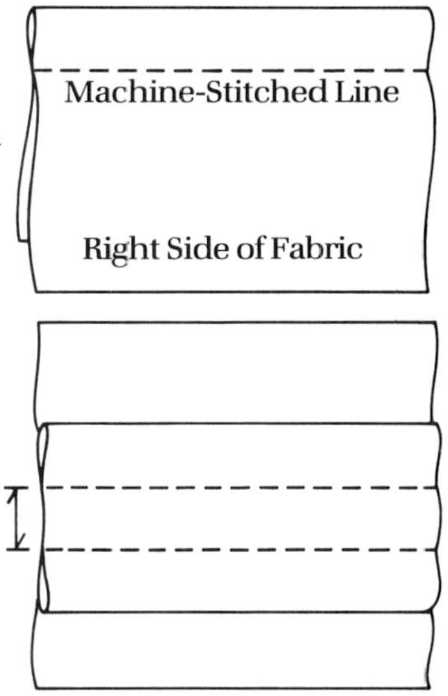

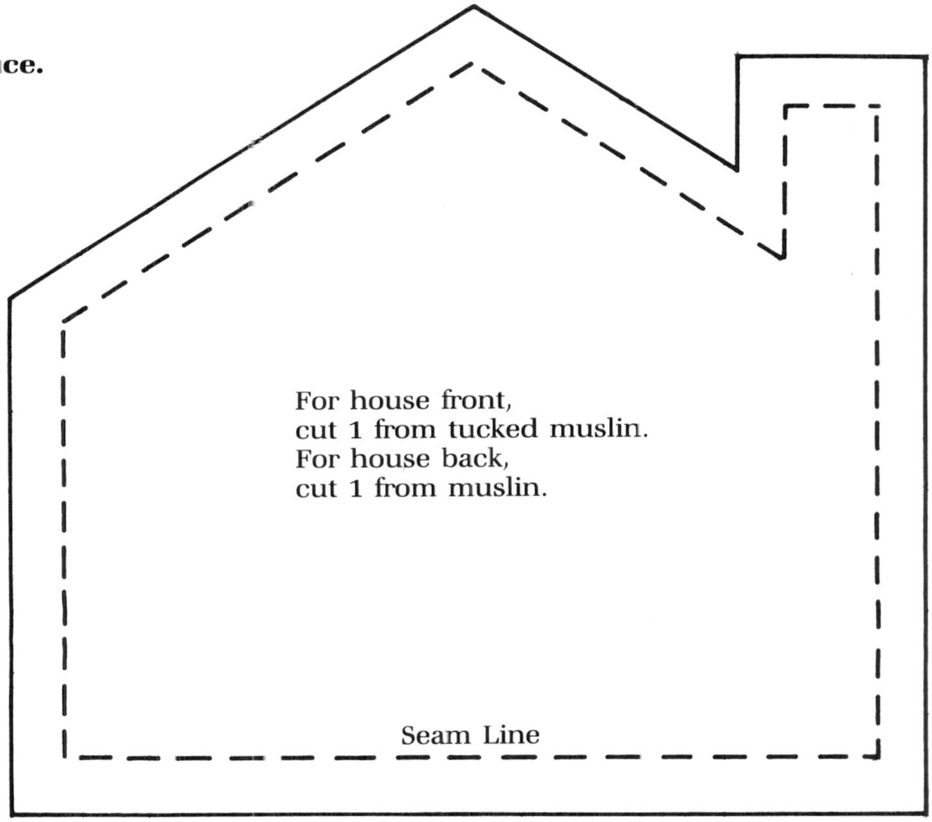

For house front,
cut 1 from tucked muslin.
For house back,
cut 1 from muslin.

Seam Line

TUCKED HOUSE ORNAMENTS

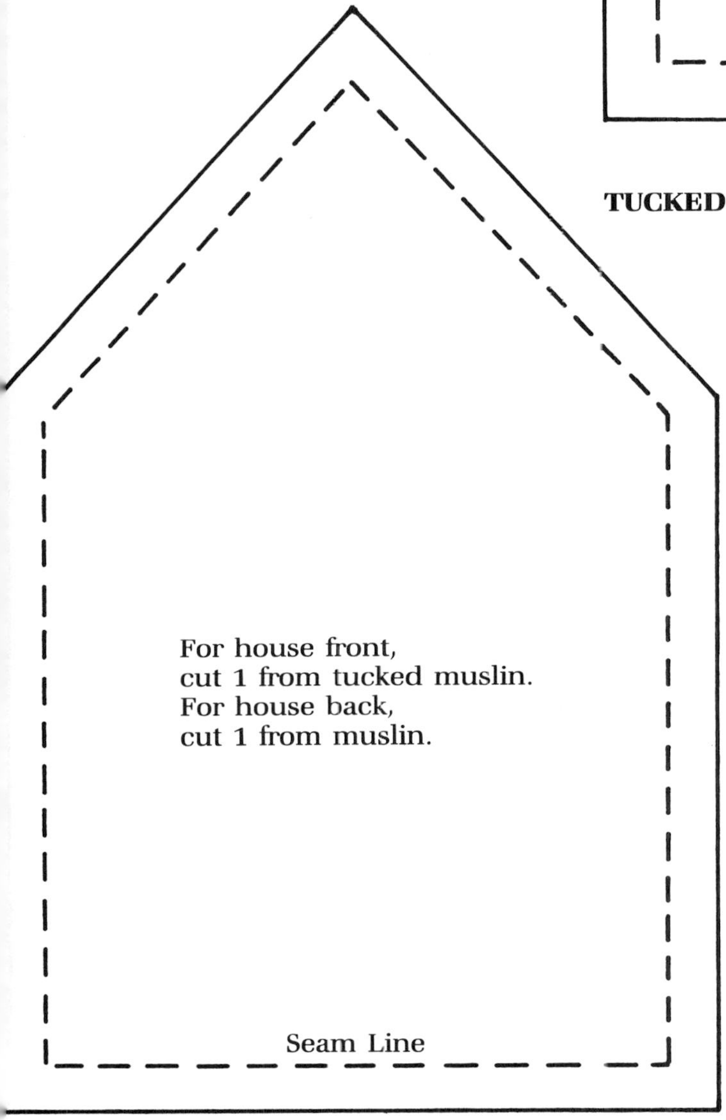

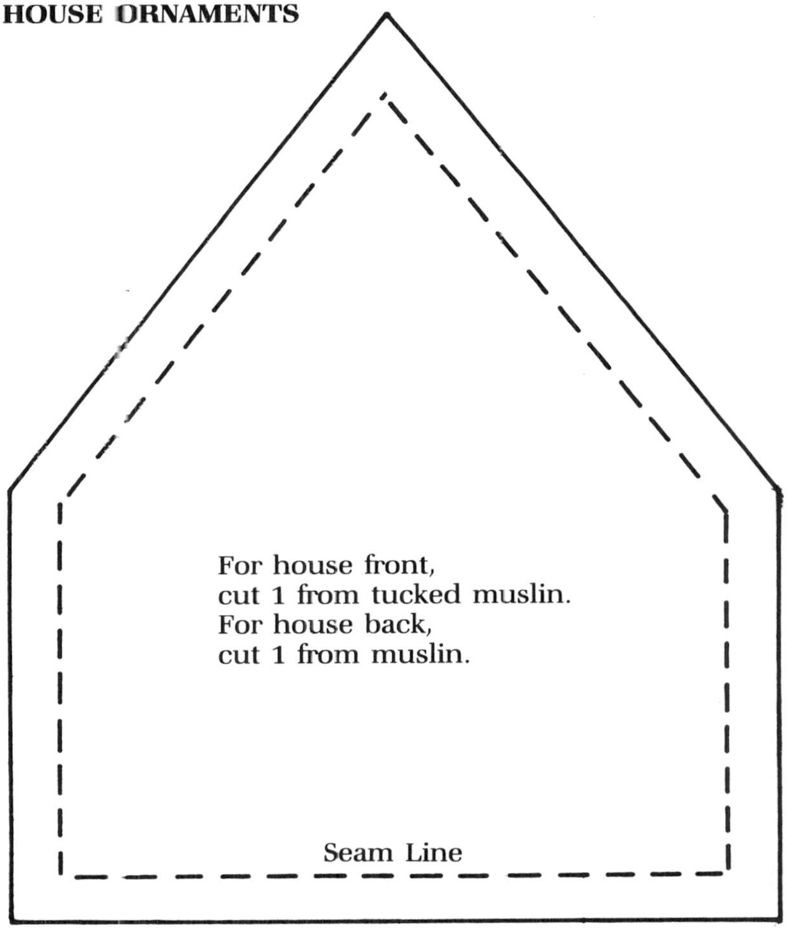

For house front,
cut 1 from tucked muslin.
For house back,
cut 1 from muslin.

Seam Line

For house front,
cut 1 from tucked muslin.
For house back,
cut 1 from muslin.

Seam Line

Variations on an Angelic Theme

Instructions are on page 48.
Patterns are full-size.
For Stitch Diagrams, see page 137.

Stitch Key (Note: Stitch Diagrams are on page 137.)

- — Straight Stitch
- — Stem Stitch
- Couched Satin Stitch
- Satin Stitch
- ✇ French Knot
- ◡ Bullion Knot
- ⊔⊔⊔ Blanket Stitch
- ᏅᏅᏅ Chain Stitch
- ⬭ Bullion Knot circled by Single Lazy Daisy Stitch
- ● Gold Bead
- ○ White Bead

Use 6 strands of floss or 3 strands of rayon thread.
Use 1 strand of gold thread.

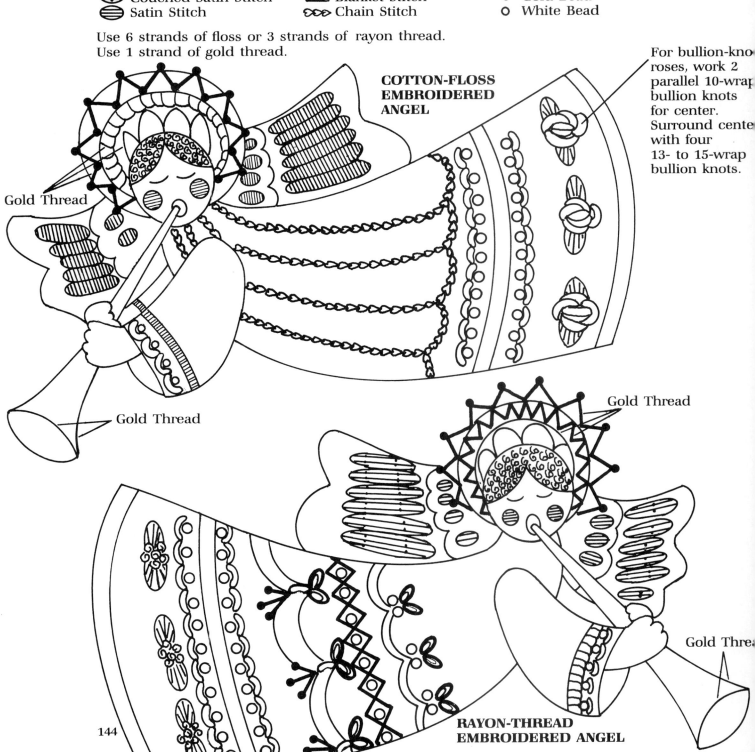

COTTON-FLOSS EMBROIDERED ANGEL

Gold Thread

Gold Thread

For bullion-kno[ts] roses, work 2 parallel 10-wrap bullion knots for center. Surround cente[r] with four 13- to 15-wrap bullion knots.

Gold Thread

Gold Thre[ad]

144

RAYON-THREAD EMBROIDERED ANGEL

Gold Thread

Serve Up Good Wishes

Instructions are on page 57.
Chart for Cross-Stitch

MERRY CHRISTMAS
CROSS-STITCH TRAY

Color Key
(Note: Numbers are for DMC floss.)

- • Gold Metallic Thread
- O 666 Red
- X 700 Green
- V 702 Light Green

Lines are straight-stitched in 700 Green.

145

Merry Christmas Critters

Instructions are on page 58.
Patterns are full-size.

EMBROIDERED RACCOON ORNAMENT
For Stitch Diagrams, see page 137.

Color Key (Note: Numbers are for DMC floss.)

Floss	Persian Yarn
1—321 Red	**9**—Dark Gray Brown
2—498 Dark Red	**10**—Medium Gray Brown
3—892 Light Red	**11**—Light Gray Brown
4—472 Pale Green	**12**—Gray Tan
5—3345 Dark Green	**13**—Gray Beige
6—699 Green	
7—310 Black	
8—White	

Stitch Key (Note: Stitch diagrams are on page 137.)

A—Satin Stitch
B—Long and Short Stitch
C—Backstitch
D—French Knot
➜ Stitch Direction

Add 1″ allowance to pattern when cutting out embroidered oval and backing piece.

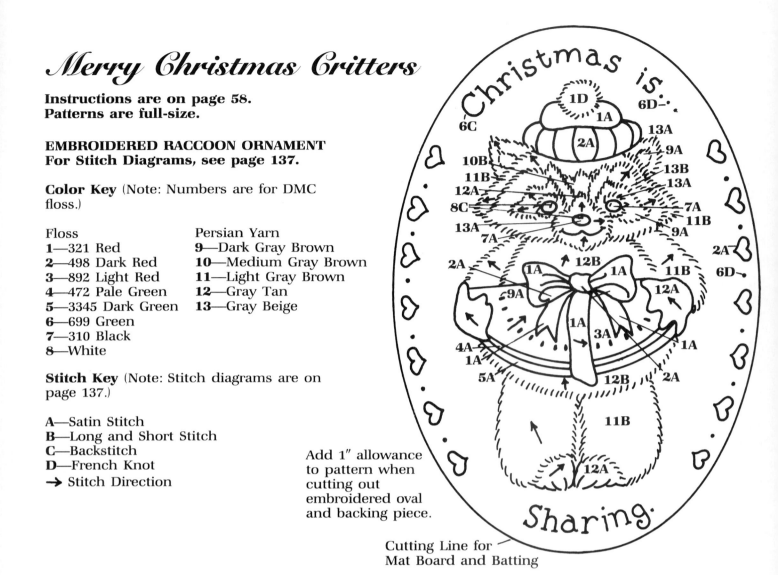

Cutting Line for Mat Board and Batting

CROSS-STITCH REDBIRD ORNAMENTS
Charts for Cross-Stitch

Color Key

Note: Numbers are for DMC floss.

-	Red Bead
	321 Red
/	741 Yellow
Z	310 Black
O	433 Brown
X	700 Green

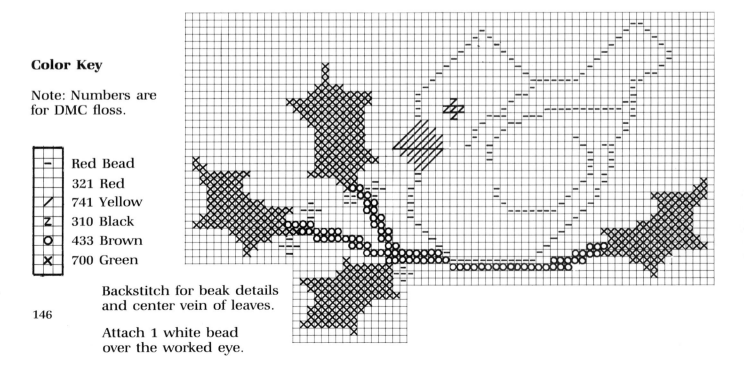

Backstitch for beak details and center vein of leaves.

Attach 1 white bead over the worked eye.

146

NEEDLEPOINT PELICAN ORNAMENTS
Chart for Needlepoint
Add ¼″ seam allowance when cutting out back piece and completed embroidery for front piece.

Color Key
Note: Numbers are for DMC floss.
1—310 Black
2—3325 Baby Blue
3—744 Pale Yellow
4—701 Light Christmas Green
5—White
6—839 Dark Beige Brown
7—842 Very Light Beige Brown
8—738 Very Light Tan
9—420 Dark Hazelnut Brown
10—938 Ultra Dark Coffee Brown
11—3022 Medium Brown Gray
12—3032 Medium Mocha Brown
13—433 Medium Brown
14—352 Light Coral
15—344 Dark Coral
16—353 Peach Flesh

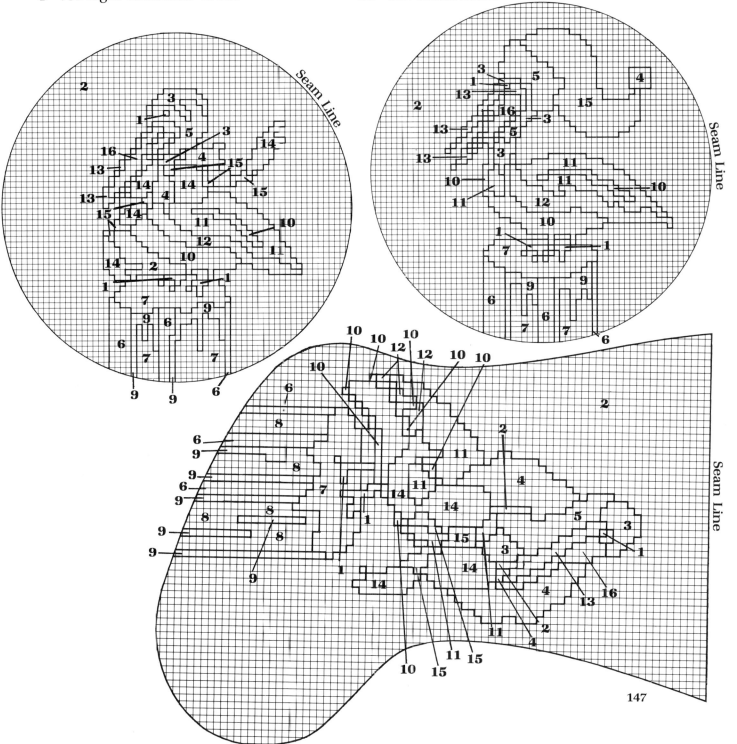

147

Strawberry Patchwork

Instructions are on page 62.
For cutting and assembly of
patchwork, follow color charts.

POT HOLDER

PLACE MAT

Color Key (Note: each square equals ¾".)
Add ½" seam allowance to each strip.

☐ Muslin
▨ Mauve
▧ Green

APRON
Skirt

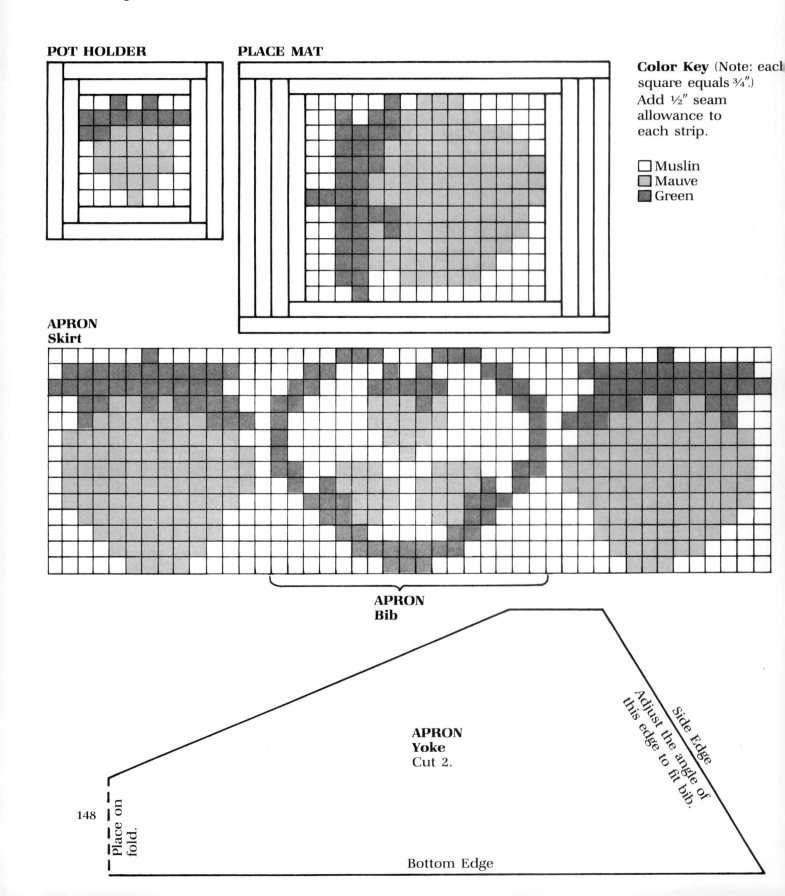

APRON
Bib

APRON
Yoke
Cut 2.

Side Edge
Adjust the angle of this edge to fit bib.

Place on fold.

148

Bottom Edge

Patterns are full-size.
Patterns include ¼″ seam allowance.

Gathering Line

Gathering Line

Small Leaf
Cut 2 for each leaf.

Gathering Line

Small Strawberry
Cut 2 for each berry.

Gathering Line

Medium Strawberry
Cut 2 for each berry.

Gathering Line

Large Leaf
Cut 2 for each leaf.

Gathering Line

Large Strawberry
Cut 2 for each berry.

Cap
Cut 1
for each
berry.

Quick-Stitch a Snowflake

Instructions are on page 75.
Pattern is full-size.
For Stitch Diagram, see page 137.

SNOWFLAKE PILLOW

¼ of pattern. Reverse and repeat for full pattern.

149

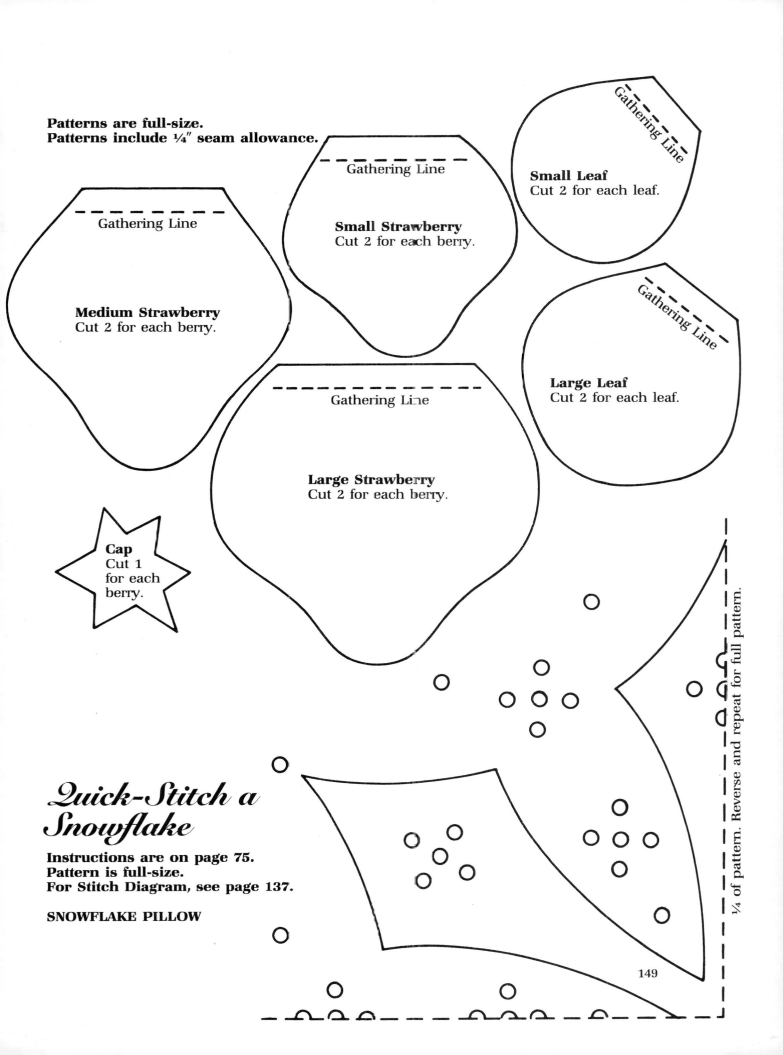

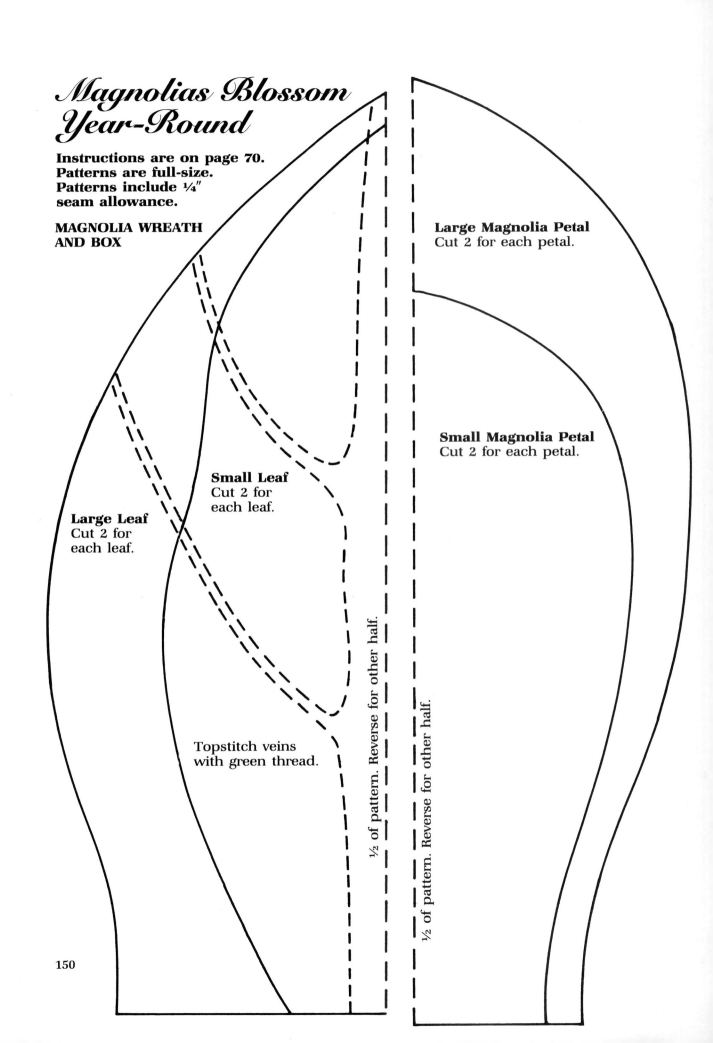

Magnolias Blossom Year-Round

Instructions are on page 70. Patterns are full-size. Patterns include ¼″ seam allowance.

MAGNOLIA WREATH AND BOX

Large Magnolia Petal
Cut 2 for each petal.

Small Magnolia Petal
Cut 2 for each petal.

Small Leaf
Cut 2 for each leaf.

Large Leaf
Cut 2 for each leaf.

Topstitch veins with green thread.

½ of pattern. Reverse for other half.

½ of pattern. Reverse for other half.

A Doll with Shaker Simplicity

Instructions are on page 68.
Patterns are full-size.
Patterns include ¼″
seam allowance.

SHAKER DOLL

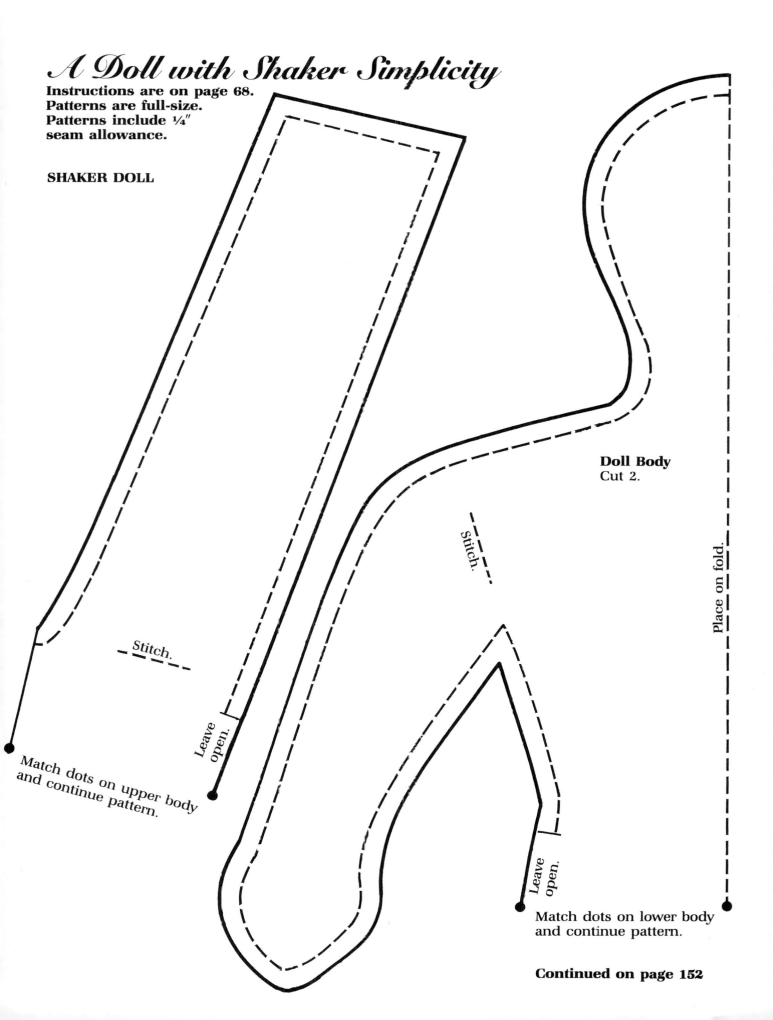

Doll Body
Cut 2.

Stitch.

Place on fold.

Stitch.

Leave open.

Leave open.

Match dots on upper body and continue pattern.

Match dots on lower body and continue pattern.

Continued on page 152

A Doll with Shaker Simplicity

(Continued)
Instructions are on page 68.
Patterns are full-size.
Patterns include ¼″
seam allowance.

SHAKER DOLL

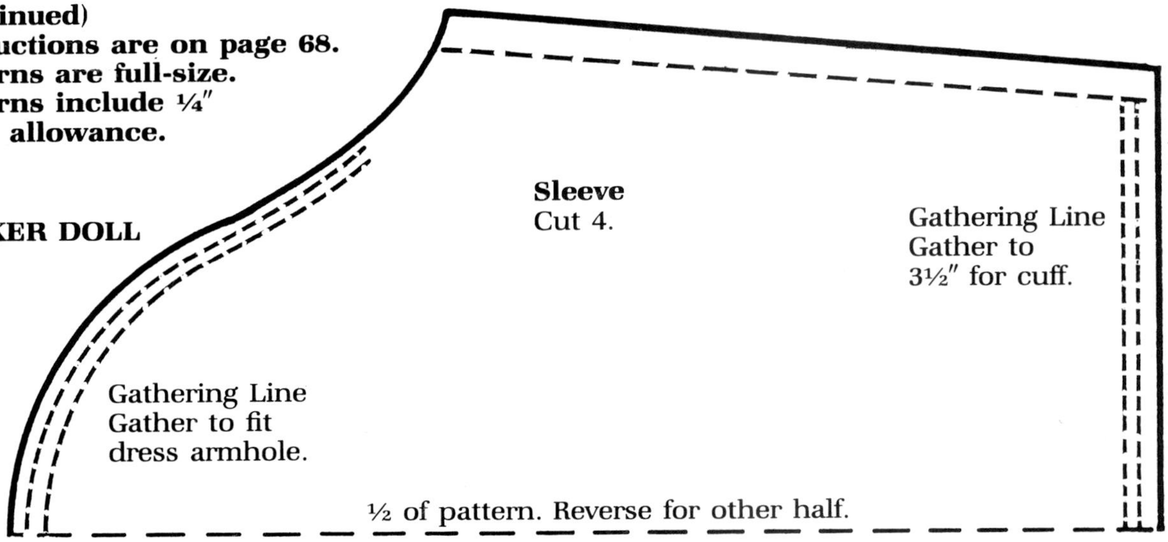

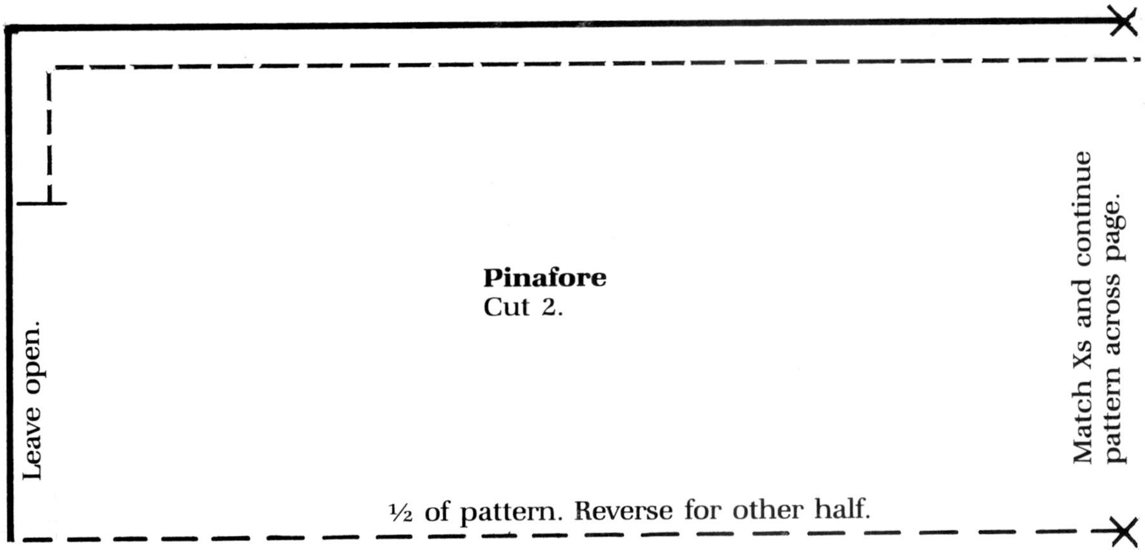

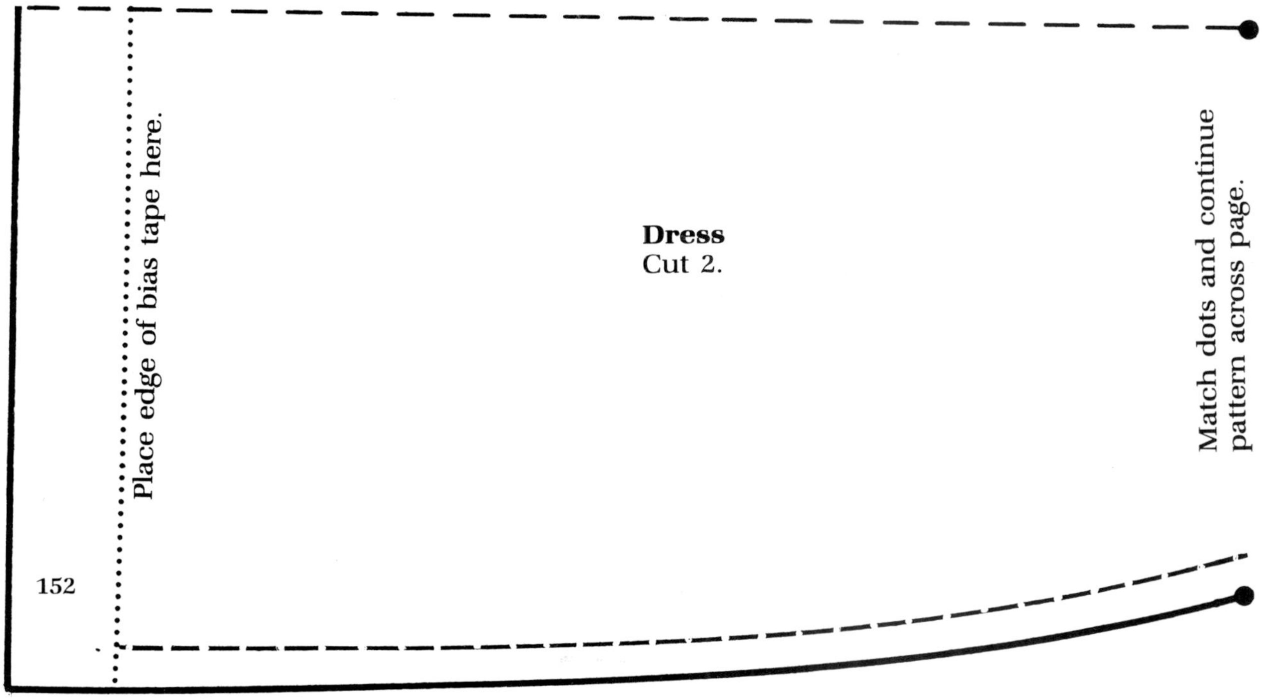

Sleeve
Cut 4.

Gathering Line
Gather to
3½″ for cuff.

Gathering Line
Gather to fit
dress armhole.

½ of pattern. Reverse for other half.

Leave open.

Pinafore
Cut 2.

Match Xs and continue pattern across page.

½ of pattern. Reverse for other half.

Place edge of bias tape here.

Dress
Cut 2.

Match dots and continue pattern across page.

152

Quilt Triangle
Cut 4 from brown wool
and 4 from blue wool.

Boot
Cut 4.

Stitch to
doll here.

Match Xs and continue
pattern across page.

Slip back straps inside front straps
and blind-stitch shoulders together.

Place on fold.

Place edge of
bias tape here.

Match dots and continue
pattern across page.

153

Gussied-Up Geese

**Instructions are on page 73.
Patterns are full-size.**

PAINTED WOODEN GOOSE

For shaded areas (above and below apron, on cheek, under eye, at tail feathers), first dip a flat brush in a diluted solution of paint and water. Then load one side of brush with undiluted paint. When making a stroke, loaded edge of brush will make the dark area of the shading.

Add a 3-dot pattern to hat, bow, and apron, (see photo) by dipping handle end of brush in paint and touching to wood surface.

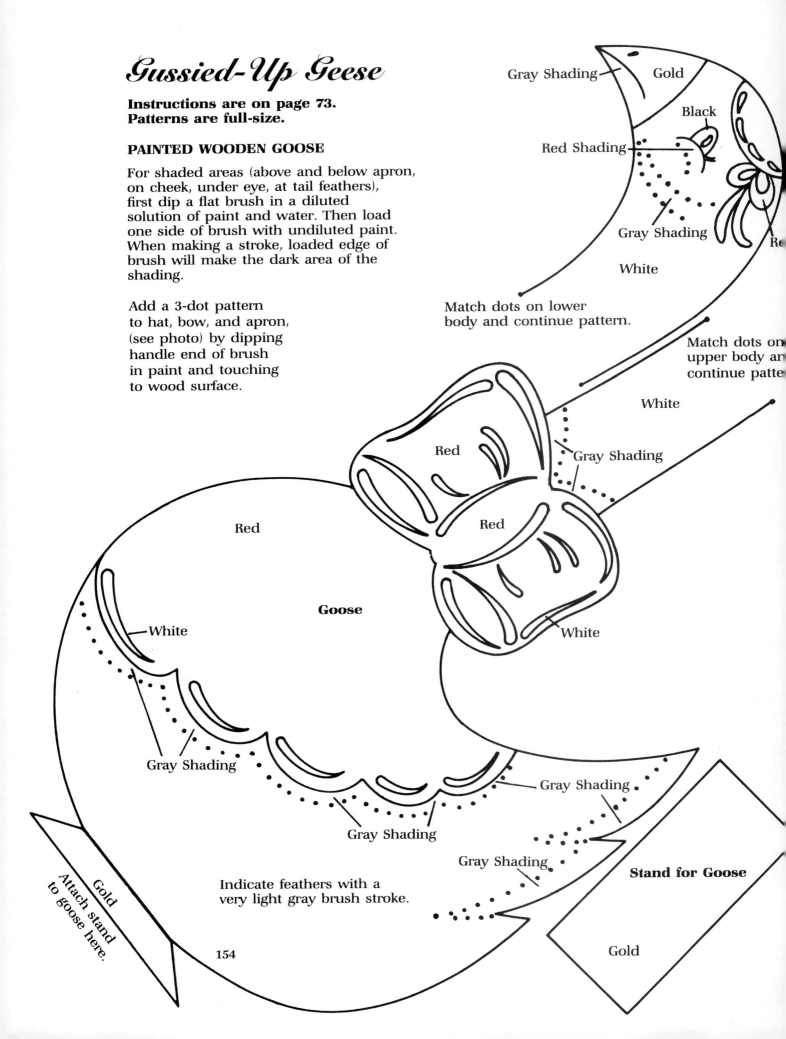

Gray Shading — Gold

Black

Red Shading

Gray Shading

White

Match dots on lower body and continue pattern.

Match dots on upper body and continue pattern

White

Red

Gray Shading

Red

Goose

White

Red

White

—White

Gray Shading

Gray Shading

Gray Shading

Gray Shading

Indicate feathers with a very light gray brush stroke.

Gold
Attach stand to goose here.

154

Stand for Goose

Gold

Contributors

Special thanks to the *Southern Living* Test Kitchens staff for preparing recipes.